JOSEPH CONRAD:
TIMES REMEMBERED

Joseph Conrad

JOSEPH CONRAD: TIMES REMEMBERED

'OJCIEC JEST TUTAJ'

JOHN CONRAD

CAMBRIDGE UNIVERSITY PRESS

CAMBRIDGE

LONDON   NEW YORK   NEW ROCHELLE
MELBOURNE   SYDNEY

920
CON

B

Published by the Press Syndicate of the University of Cambridge
The Pitt Building, Trumpington Street, Cambridge CB2 1RP
32 East 57th Street, New York, NY 10022, USA
296 Beaconsfield Parade, Middle Park, Melbourne 3206, Australia

© Cambridge University Press 1981

First published 1981

Set, printed and bound in Great Britain by
Fakenham Press Limited, Fakenham, Norfolk

British Library Cataloguing in Publication Data
Conrad, John
Joseph Conrad, times remembered.
1. Conrad, Joseph – biography
2. Novelists, English – 20th century – biography
I. Title
823'.9'12   PR6005.04Z/   79–41596
ISBN 0 521 22805 0

Contents

To the memory of Richard Curle
and friends of my father

Illustrations

*(Unless otherwise stated the illustrations are from the author's private
collection.)*

Preface

Soon after we arrived at the hotel in Vienna in the late afternoon of 9 October 1914 my father asked me to take a message to some Polish friends who were also staying there. He took me into the corridor and said, 'When you have found their room, knock on the door and say, "Ojciec jest tutaj". Now don't forget, "Ojciec jest tutaj" – it means "father is here".'

I have not forgotten. The words themselves will not mean much to the many people who admire my father's works, but over the years of writing down these memories they have acquired a special meaning for me, and I feel that I am in duty bound to include them as a subtitle.

To those who read these reminiscences, which are a true record of the last fifteen years of my father's life, I can only hope that they will be aware of my father's presence in these pages.

Neither my mother, my brother nor I ever learnt to speak Polish but I still remember the few words and sentences which my father taught me, and in those words are many recollections of the years that have passed. When I tell an anecdote to friends their response is always 'Why don't you write it down?' Among my many friends, Richard Curle was the most insistent and whenever we met he took me to task, saying, 'You really ought to write your reminiscences. Get them down on paper. They give a picture of your father that no other person can give. You owe it to your father; he would expect it of you.'

I can recall in my mind's eye the picture of his room at West Coker, lit by a single bright bulb in a dark shade, as we talked far into the night. In the shadow his figure, reclining in a deep armchair, his face and eyes appearing every now and then when lit by the glow of his cigarette. For a while I was silent then said, 'Dick, you may laugh at me but many years ago when I realised JC's position in the world of letters, I decided that I would not intrude into that world. So many people have written about his work that I feel that any contribution that I may make could well be superfluous.'

He said, leaning forward and gazing into the fire, 'It could be so but then your recollections would be personal, more authentic about your father. You know far more about him as a person and a father than anyone else because you seem to have spent more time in his company, especially in the later years. By time I mean the actual hours and minutes when you were together but of course in "years" you knew him for the shortest time. You have told me a lot about him that I did not know but which I had assumed, and although I knew him well I know him better now. I only knew the family life of a generous host who always made a fuss of me, but now the picture is complete. You know as well as I do that very few books have been written about your father himself. About his books, yes, and we must be very grateful that his work has created so much interest though some of the books, one suspects, were written more for their author's edification than to appraise JC's ability.'

Eventually he persuaded me that I ought to make the effort, and over the years I jotted down various recollections, but it was not until I gave a talk on my father that I cast aside the last lingering doubts. I had never promised JC, and nor had he asked me, to keep quiet. I am convinced that it never occurred to him, not seriously at any rate, that any of us would write about him. He encouraged my mother to write her cookery book but never tried to persuade me to write at any time.

A year or so later I sent my first effort to Richard Curle for criticism and received a long letter of valuable advice pointing out that I had hardly mentioned my father's friends and only referred to himself en passant. He wrote: 'You have chosen an apt title but you must realise that your father's friends are an important part of his life and, while I do not pretend to have influenced him, I am part of that life – an important part if what you have told me is true about your father's references to me.' Dear Dick, he forgave me but I felt even more inadequate for the task and time passed all too quickly. His sudden death in 1968 was a great shock and loss after a friendship which had lasted over fifty years. But time moves on and all that is history now.

A feeling of adventure mixed with trepidation was the sensation that I had when I first put pen to paper to record these recollections. One's inadequacy seems to hover over the blank page, anxiety flickers on the horizon like summer lightning and doubt lurks in each full stop and comma. Have I the ability to do justice to the subject? Can I justify my father's trust in me?

It is so easy to embroider memories, but I shall try not to do so, from the earliest days in the cottage at Aldington through the years at Capel House, the brief period at Spring Grove and the last four years at Oswalds. I hope I shall be able to convey the interest shown and the companionship given by an understanding and, perhaps, over-generous father, who nevertheless impressed upon me at a very early age that 'I must justify my existence on this earth, be honest with myself and with all men, be confident but not conceited.'

Recalling some fifteen years of memories from the age of three to eighteen it seems logical to arrange them in defined periods of time but not strictly in chronological order within those periods. Also I found it easier to recall the past by dividing my reminiscences into the following intervals:

> Aldington, 1909–10, the infant
> Capel House, 1910–14, the child
> Capel House, 1914–19, the boy
> Spring Grove and Oswalds, 1919–24, the youth

Apart from checking dates in the *Life and Letters* edited by Jean Aubry (2 volumes, Heinemann, London, 1927) I have not read any books about my father's works for a number of years. Nor have I read my brother's book or those by my mother, as I want to record only the events which I remember personally. I shall call attention to events about which I was told in later years but otherwise I shall relate events as I remember them. For a fuller account of the life and work of my father I would refer the reader to Jocelyn Baines's book *Joseph Conrad: a critical biography* (Weidenfeld and Nicolson, London, 1960), and to Norman Sherry's books, *Conrad's Eastern World* and *Conrad's Western World* (Cambridge University Press, 1966 and 1971). From time to time I mention my grandparents and my father's dislike of Russians. The brief explanation is that my grandparents, along with my father, were exiled to Siberia for being involved in protests against the tyranny of the Tsars and the ruling classes, and that my father's mother was brutally forced to travel back to Siberia when she was obviously dying of consumption; orders were given that no mercy should be shown to her or my father and they were sent back to an area where there was no medical attention whatever. For further explanation the reader is referred to *Under Western Eyes*, and to two essays by my father 'Autocracy and War' and 'The Crime of Partition' (J. M. Dent and Sons, uniform edition, London, 1921).

I shall refer to my father as JC though I did not address him in this way until much later, about 1920, when we were living at Oswalds. As a child I called him 'Dada' when the need arose but never 'Dad' or 'Father'. My mother would tell me to take things to 'your father' but to me it never seemed a suitable form of address, not that he was aloof or distant (except when annoyed). He was a most approachable person but he expected good manners and had no time for anyone who butted in when other people were speaking.

Aldington days, 1909–10

I

The infant. Early recollections – pretending illness –
the cure – the cottage – Mr and Mrs Post – playing
on the bank – Mr Slingsby – the iron horse – cuts
and bruises – clean and tidy for meals

When my parents left 'The Someries', near Luton in Bedfordshire, it
was to return to Kent, to a tiny cottage at the bottom of Ruffins Hill
at Aldington. It was a dark and gloomy place rendered more so by
the dark paint which seemed to be the usual colour for dwellings at
that time. Add to this the fact that it was built on the north side of an
abrupt hill which effectively cut off any sunlight from early autumn
to late spring, and one had all the ingredients for a thoroughly
depressing abode. It was primitive in the extreme: water from a well
outside the back door, a bucket in a shed at the end of the garden as a
toilet, and fires that produced more smoke than heat, hardly created
the atmosphere in which to write anything, let alone masterpieces of
literature.

The darkness of the cottage forms the background for my few and
rather sketchy recollections of that time, dominated in a strange way
by the silhouette of the frame and bars of the window through which
I remember seeing the branches of a tree against the sky. The stairs
were very steep and narrow, without any daylight, but there was a
rope which helped to lead one up to the tiny landing and the two
bedrooms.

I still remember, vividly, sitting on a wooden chair with my feet on
another chair, a blue rug with red lines forming a squared pattern
thrown over my legs, groaning and trying to snap my fingers as I had
seen my father do when he had an attack of gout. My mother, passing
through the room on her way upstairs, would stop and say: 'I think
you ought to find something better to do.' I suppose it was a normal
reaction for a child to what must have seemed the very frequent
attention that my father needed when he was ill.

The game of 'being ill' was cured but the memory of that unhappy morning has remained with me ever since. We had a daily help as my mother was lame even in those days and suffered a lot of pain from her damaged knee. One day when my father was ill she had to go out, presumably to fetch the doctor, and I was left alone with the daily help. Whether it was devilment on my part, or boredom, is immaterial, but when my mother had gone I sat myself down on a chair with my feet on another with the rug thrown over my knees, twiddling my thumbs and groaning. Suddenly I was seized by the arm, dragged up the stairs and thrust into my father's bedroom where he was lying in bed, his throat so swollen that from where I stood I could only just see his forehead. I broke free of the grip that held me and clambered down the stairs followed by the 'ogre'. When I hear, in a coarse and raucous voice, 'That'll teach yer', those awful moments come rushing back and the memories of nightmares peopled with beings with vastly swollen throats jostle for attention in my mind.

When my mother returned she was very worried by my scared appearance but I was too frightened to tell her what had happened. I could feel the eyes of the daily help following me about the room warning me not to say anything. I never told my mother but somehow she found out and we very soon had a different daily help. My mother must have realised what had happened because as soon as the swelling of my father's throat had gone down I was taken in to see him. Thoughtless as the action was it cured me of playing at being ill!

The cottage was the northern one of a pair on the east side of the lane that passes through a small group of cottages and houses dominated by the church which is surrounded by the remains of an archiepiscopal palace, in the original village of Aldington. The next-door cottage was occupied by a butcher, but the only other thing I can remember about him was that his name was Dryland.

About eighty yards up the hill on the other side of the lane stood a row of cottages along the top of a bank, the nearest one of which was the home of Mr and Mrs Post, an elderly couple of country folk with whom my parents seemed to get on well. On fine evenings the three of us would walk up the hill, climb the rough steps cut into the bank and arrive on the square paved area in front of their cottage. My parents used to sit on the low wall that ran round two sides of the paving where it was pleasantly cool in hot weather as it faced east towards the farm on the other side of the lane where Mr Slingsby lived. The church could just be seen to the right behind the farm buildings and the evening sun made the old stone walls and tiled roofs glow with a golden warmth.

My mother sat on the wall that stuck out from the front of the cottage with her injured leg laid along it, while JC sat facing the doorway. Mr Post leant against the jamb of the doorway behind his wife who sat bolt upright on a wooden chair to which she seemed to be rigidly fixed by glue. Her hands rested on her lap, her head remained quite still as her eyes moved from one to the other of my parents as they spoke. Their lack of movement must have been exceptional because my memory of them is more of two dummies than of two people; in fact the only movement on their part was made by Mr Post removing the stump of clay pipe from his mouth when he was going to say something. It was bizarre, four people sitting almost motionless carrying on a conversation in quiet unemotional tones while a child scrambled about on the bank or leant against one of his parents. In the autumn, when the chestnuts had fallen from the nearby tree, JC would play catch with me, or tell me to set up an old tin and supply him with chestnuts to throw into it, which he did with great skill while the quiet conversation continued.

JC often took me with him when he went to get butter and eggs from the farmer, Mr Slingsby, whose farm was further up the hill between us and the church. It was typical of many Kentish farms of the period, well drained – into the gutter at the side of the road – the stockyard always deep in straw and mud. What mud! To be fair it was no worse than other farms and it only drained down the road in very wet weather. A line of large squared stones from the nearby ruins had been laid from the farmyard gate to the door of the house so that it was possible to arrive indoors without bringing too much of the countryside in as well.

Before setting out for the farm JC would put on a pair of boots, then a pair of leather gaiters, all of which had to be spotlessly clean. My attire was a pair of blue serge shorts, a blue jersey, dark blue or black stockings and black boots, likewise spotlessly clean and polished. If it was cold we put on overcoats, and whatever the weather JC always wore a hat. We would walk up the hill and turn left along the cart track, open the yard gate and negotiate the stepping stones and arrive at the farmhouse door to be greeted by Mr Slingsby or his wife.

I was always surprised at seeing Mr Slingsby come across the muddy yard without getting his boots and leggings dirty; they were every bit as clean as JC's. Looking back it was as if the two men vied with each other to see who could keep clean and free from mud the longest. My father was very particular about his dress and was always well turned out but Mr Slingsby, on the other hand, apart from his boots and leggings, was not so particular. He wore knee-breeches, generously patched, and a Norfolk jacket, discoloured and also patched. Under this he wore a corduroy 'Westkit' in which reposed a massive watch, a real old turnip attached to a length of leather bootlace knotted into a buttonhole. On his head was a battered and stained cloth hat with several brightly coloured feathers stuck in behind the ribbon. Below the hat a pair of deep-set bright eyes in a weather-beaten face gave one a friendly look. His face was framed by a fringe of dark hair down each side and under the chin and, although much lined, appeared to be a young face with a smile lurking round the mouth. I have been told he was quite a character and JC spent a lot of time talking to him, though about what I have no idea. It would not have been about farming as that was of no interest to my father, likewise gossip or scandal had no attraction for him. It could have been about the Romney Marsh which stretched away from the foot of the hills about two miles south of Aldington.

Only a few friends came to see us here as it was about two miles across the fields and along the lane to Smeeth station; about seven miles to Hythe and eight miles to Ashford, from all of which one had to complete the journey in a horse and trap or, later, in a taxi.

There are only two friends of my father who stand out in my memory of those days. The first, Percival Gibbon, brought his family to live in a half-timbered cottage on the other side of the lane a little to the north of us. The other, Ford Madox Hueffer, lived about half a mile away across the fields at a house called Postling Green, which stands on the south side of the road to Lympne on the edge of the South Downs overlooking the Romney Marsh. On clear days the town of Rye with its hill-top church can be seen away to the south-west.

My mother often took me down the lane and across the field to see Maisie Gibbon. She walked very slowly with a stick because her damaged kneecap, the result of a fall some years earlier, gave her continual pain. The surgeon to whom she was taken tried to bend the knee over a bar, doing even more harm, and causing her excruciating pain. She kept me by her side while we were in the lane although we hardly ever saw any traffic, only an occasional farm-cart or a pony and trap, but as soon as we turned off the lane I was allowed to run on ahead. Down the rough stony track I'd rush, ignoring advice to take care, stumble on a stone and fall, grazing my knee. Doubtless there was a hullabaloo, soap and warm water, iodine and bandages, and finally a very subdued small boy being told to thank Auntie Maisie for tidying up the mess. There were many occasions when Mrs Gibbon came to my rescue and I have often thought since how patient she was when 'mother earth came up and hit me'. Her own two girls were much steadier on their feet. It may seem as though my mother did not care but I am sure she did. It was much easier for an able person to get the bandages and bring relief. The crushed flint surfaces of the roads and tracks of those days have gone; it was quite uncomfortable having the little sharp slivers of flint washed out from knees, hands and elbows, and sometimes it was three or four days before they had all been removed.

It was Hueffer who offered my father the cottage at Aldington, as a sub-tenant, as he, Hueffer, had moved to Postling Green. I am grateful to him for an arrangement which enabled my parents to get back to Kent and away from the Someries where Hueffer had led them a pretty dance. I was too young to notice but it must have been quite a circus for my mother. My first recollection of Hueffer is of being put into my high-chair opposite him at a meal-time where, it is more than likely, I gazed at him in an 'owlish' way as children sometimes do. It was not long before he took the offensive by trying to make me misbehave and then complain to my mother about the 'ill-mannered little brat'. After a number of similar incidents I was given my food in the kitchen. I do not remember ever hearing my parents remonstrate with Hueffer. Apart from these encounters I do not recall seeing him at the cottage though he must have been a fairly frequent visitor. I expect I was kept discreetly out of the way for it was not until we went to live at Capel House that I became aware of him again.

Other friends came, such as Garnett and Hope, but with these kindly and considerate people nothing happened to leave a memory, so their visits must have been happy ones, which is understandable, as they were very peaceful companions.

As a reward for being good or, perhaps, as a means of getting me to bed, my father used to make me one or two paper boats while I sat on

Borys and John Conrad while at Aldington, 1909–10

his knee. When they were finished I would thank him, give him a kiss, scramble down and rush off to the kitchen where a large enamelled tin bath would be waiting in front of the cooker. My mother supervised my undressing while the daily help poured in the hot water from an enormous kettle which was always kept simmering on the stove. A bucket or so of cold water was added until the temperature was about right and I was allowed to get in. Sometimes JC would come to see how the boats floated, at other times he would be called to look at some masterpiece of a bruise or a deep scratch. After making an inspection he would reassure my mother by saying he had seen worse. Bruises were always treated with arnica and brown paper while scratches, after being bathed, were dabbed with iodine and bandaged if necessary.

My father was most particular that I should be presentable at meal-times: clothes clean and tidy, hands washed and hair brushed. It was a rule that I should not get down from the table at the end of a meal without asking permission. If I forgot I was immediately called back and made to sit quite still for five minutes. 'Quite still' meant just that, hands, head and feet all had to be kept motionless and my father would get very angry with anyone who tried to make me move by tickling me or any other trick. There were frequent rows with Hueffer when he deliberately tried to make me move or behave badly. It seemed to me that his one aim was to make trouble for me. If I did not respond he suggested that I was 'dim' and if I did, he pounced on me for bad behaviour.

My parents took me with them whenever they went out as there was no one with whom they felt they could leave me, and so I was with them one dark and windy evening as we returned to the cottage. We had turned off the Ashford to Folkestone road into the lane and were approaching the tunnel through the railway embankment when a train passed over, travelling towards Folkestone and throwing up a shower of sparks from its funnel. JC, sitting in front by the driver, turned round and patted me on the knee saying: 'Look, Jackilo, see the train with the iron horse.' For a long time after that I was most disappointed when our little pony, pulling the trap home through the dark, did not give off a shower of sparks – only one or two when her hoof struck a stone. Whenever I pass under a railway when a train is passing overhead, I remember that evening sitting close to my mother wrapped in a rug, JC and the driver outlined against the glare of the lights and the darkness receding as we moved on into the night, along the white grit surface with broad green verges enclosed by high hedges giving the impression of an endless cavern.

Towards the end of our stay at the cottage we made afternoon trips in the little pony-trap behind Jenny, the small brown mare, to Capel House to which we were going to move. I was looking forward to the move as there was a long moat on the east side and lots of trees and ponds as well as woodlands. I was also to have a playroom which I was to share with my mother.

Capel House days, 1910–14

2

The child. Capel House – garden – interior – galley
– Nellie Lyons – Mrs C cooking – knots – emissary
– toys – talks after tea – nautical – geographical –
Lear – Æsop's *Fables* – faces in the bark of trees

When we lived at Capel House, Orlestone, it was surrounded by
fields with woodlands stretching beyond on three sides. There were
many ponds in the fields and most of them contained islands of
willow saplings, inhabited by moorhen, wild ducks and water rats.
Along the east and west boundaries of the garden were some well-
established Scots firs, and on the south side these were joined by an
old hawthorn hedge along the roadside, while on the north side a
post-and-rail fence completed the boundary. There was a small
orchard of fruit trees to the west of the house, and a large kitchen
garden at the rear.

Capel was one of the few moated farmhouses in this part of Kent,
built on a mound with a moat all round it some fifteen to twenty feet
wide and eight to ten feet deep. There were two points of access
where the ground had not been excavated, and originally, across
these, fieldgates were set with wings going down into the water of the
moat. Towards the end of the last century cattle or sheep were driven
within the confines of the moat and the gates shut as a protection
from the bands of thieves who roved in the surounding woods. Only
the eastern side of the moat held water, about three feet deep, the
southern and western parts had been partly filled in and a copper-
beech hedge had been planted halfway up the outer slope. The
northern part of the moat was clearly defined but only after a long
spell of rainy weather did it contain any water.

The house was built of locally-made red bricks with a Kentish
tiled roof, set rather low, which gave one the impression that it was
crouching close to the ground. It was rather a dark house but it had
an air of friendliness on which my father often commented. There
was a small field between the roadside hedge and the southern moat

round which the drive curved to approach the south-west corner of the house where it divided, one part went straight ahead to the drive sweep before the front door, and the other part went along the back of the house turned left past the sheds, then over the north moat and westward to the oast house.

The front door led into a small square hall from which a door opened into the dining room, and opposite this was the door into the drawing room where my father worked. It was the lightest room in the house with a large bay window facing south and a long high-set shallow window facing east which let in the morning sun. My father's desk was placed across the corner between the windows and he had only to lift his head to see most of the front garden. In the other corners of the dining room were the doors leading to the 'crew's' quarters. The den which I shared with my mother lay along a dark passage to the left, while straight ahead was the back hall, with the kitchen on the left, the long room or ''tween decks' on the right with the pantry and larder at the far end. The kitchen or 'galley', as JC always called it, had a small window facing north with a stone sink under it and in the corner to the right was a pump which the gardener used each morning to fill the tank in the roof. The cooker was set in a deep recess opposite the window and both it and the recess were conscientiously blackleaded each week so that 'the soot marks didn't show'! The walls and ceiling were a dingy brown, gradually darkened by the occasional smoking of the stove, in spite of being whitewashed each spring. The long room or ''tween decks' was used for all the odd jobs, and for storing firewood and logs in the cold weather. The pantry, larder, or 'lazaret' could hardly have been further away from the galley, being tucked away in the north-east corner of the house. On wet days, when I was hard up for something to do, I would be called upon to be a galley-slave, fetching and carrying things from the lazaret to the galley for my mother. Looking back one is amazed at the lack of thought that meant we put up with this arrangement when there was ample room for a larder next to the galley by the back door.

There were doors from the ''tween decks' and the dining room onto the small dark landing at the foot of the stairs that rose up between two walls to a slightly less dark first-floor landing lit by a window at the top of the attic stairs. Immediately on the left at the top of the stairs was the door to my parents' bedroom, and in the opposite corner of this room was the door to my bedroom, which was

Joseph Conrad at his desk, Capel House

long and narrow, being under the slope of the roof over the drawing
room, and was lit by a small window over the bay window below. My
bed was placed as far as possible from the window and it was such a
dark room that I had to have a candle by which to undress, even in
midsummer. Often before falling asleep I would lie and listen to the
murmur of voices as my parents talked in the room below but I could
not hear what was said as the floor was too well made. Over the den
was the spare room which also served as a sick bay when anyone was
ill; and next to this was the WC with a most original and erratic
method of flushing. In the bottom of the tank in the roof, immediately over the pipe to the WC, a cork was suspended on the end of an
iron rod by a length of cord which terminated at a ring handle in the
WC. If one pulled the ring the right amount and then released it, all
was well and the cork was sucked into the pipe with a resounding
thud, but if one pulled too hard the tank emptied. The local plumber

was persuaded by JC to put a 'stop' on the cord to prevent the cork from being pulled too far.

Next door was my brother's room above the kitchen and then came a replica of the long room below, part of which had been partitioned off to make a bathroom and passage to the maid's room at the far end. It was a bathroom in name only; we had to provide a round tin bath, carry the hot water up from the kitchen and, when finished, carry the water down again. Later a cast-iron bath was fitted, with a waste, but we still had to carry the water upstairs.

In addition to the cooker in the kitchen there were three other fires to be lit each morning – the dining room, drawing room and den and, if anyone was staying or was ill, the spare room as well. All these fires had been lit and burning well by the time we came down for breakfast at about nine o'clock.

My parents had decided to have a maid living in when we moved to Capel to help with the housework and look after me when my mother was busy typing my father's manuscripts. So Nellie Lyons came to live with us. She was one of a large family and not very strong, suffering from a digestive complaint and always feeling cold. Like so many young people in those days her schooling had been very elementary since the circumstances of the family made it necessary for her to earn a living from an early age. What she lacked in health and strength was made up for by her devotion to us. She was always willing and anxious to help, though there were times when my mother found her lack of attention rather trying. She would be asked to fetch one thing from the larder and would go bustling off only to return with something quite different. This 'wandering' by Nellie was probably due to feeling unwell and, although the doctor frequently prescribed for her, nothing seemed to provide more than a temporary relief.

My mother did all the cooking, sewing and typing while Nellie did the housework so I was left very much to my own devices. JC gave me toys or money to buy them and whenever he went away made a point of bringing me some little thing on his return. On rainy days or during the long winter evenings he would get up from the tea table and say: 'If you've nothing better to do, get a length of rope and bring it to me.' My mother would find a length of cord which I would take to him, be lifted onto his knee, and then he would proceed to make various knots: half-hitch, reef, bowline, slippery hitch, and others, all made with deceptive ease. Then it was my turn to try; eventually I could make most of them without assistance but never blindfolded or behind my back as JC could. I was never aware that he became impatient though he did get a bit 'short' with some people who, through nervousness, became mentally slow. People were a bit nervous meeting JC for the first time but he had the knack of making people at ease and always listened with attention to what they had to say.

When the weather limited my outdoor activities my mother found it very distracting to have me dodging around her while she tried to decipher a series of corrections in a manuscript. I soon tired of watching the letter drum of the Blickensderfer typewriter bobbing and spinning as the page moved past and was bored long before the first page was handed to me to pile up. However she soon thought of a way of keeping me occupied and saving herself a lot of walking, always a painful business, while getting the corrections sorted out. There were massive thresholds at each of the three doorways between the den and the drawing room so she would type her interpretations of the various corrections on a scrap of paper which she then gave to me to take to my father. I would knock on the door of the drawing room and be told to enter, walk up to my father's desk, bring my heels smartly together, bow from the hips and say: 'May it please, your excellency, to receive these papers.'

JC would take them and say: 'Please be seated while I attend to them.'

This somewhat cold procedure came about one day when I had brought him some papers while my mother had been getting tea ready. He lifted me onto his knee and explained that I was to be an 'emissary' between him and my mother and went on to explain how an emissary should behave, never fidgeting while waiting and always showing respect by being quiet. When he had finished writing his instructions for my mother he would ask me to give his warmest regards to my immediate superior, as he handed them back to me.

Of course there were those occasions when he resented being interrupted, when I would be told to 'get out', as he stormed through the house into the den, waving the offending piece of paper and demanding to know: 'Why has the King's English become incomprehensible, eh?' or 'Has my handwriting become so bad that it cannot be read?' This was very unfair as there might be three or four different versions of a passage from which my mother had to choose the right one. Often he would 'try out' different groups of words and omit to cross out those that did not come up to the standard or create the meaning he wished to achieve. He always regretted these flare-ups and would apologise later.

My father had his 'off' days when everything seemed to go wrong but these periods did not predominate in our lives though minor misdemeanours on my part tended to attract attention. When I had misbehaved he gave me a severe talking to and explained why I should not do things that I had been told not to do. This 'dressing down' was given at the time of the offence but never in front of strangers or guests. I would be taken outside the room and reprimanded and then sent back to apologise if necessary. When I went in to say 'Goodnight' I was forgiven for any shortcomings during the day, sometimes with a repetition of the reasons for the 'ticking off' but there was never any going on about it. The lesson was learnt and that closed the matter.

JC did not insist that I should join him in his room after tea. That was for me to decide, and if I had something I wanted to play with in the den the chances were that he would come to see what it was and would often spend quite a while giving advice or helping me in some way. Like all small boys I had my boxes of soldiers and a variety of field guns and howitzers but JC did not take any interest in them or encourage me in having 'battles'. It is very doubtful whether he had any toys of that kind even if my grandfather's guards allowed them.

The after-tea talks were not regular features of our life and some-times a week would go by before he suggested that I should join him in his room. In addition to nautical instruction with ropes, an evening might be spent on geography, talking about rivers, mountains, deserts and forests, or about the people and wild animals in foreign lands. At other times it would be on elementary geology, rocks and the formation of the earth's crust, or on the weather and the probable results of various cloud formations. His knowledge of seamanship, navigation and meteorology must have been more extensive than most ships' captains and his ability to make it interesting to a small boy was most impressive. Prehistoric animals had a great fascination for him and I have only to look at the illustrations in the Reverend Hutchinson's book *Creatures of other days*, to be back in the drawing room at Capel House sitting on my father's knee while he turned the pages and described how the pictures were created from bits of skeletons and fossils.

Evelina Korzeniowska, the mother of Joseph Conrad

Apollo Korzeniowski, the father of Joseph Conrad

When I was a bit older he read to me from Edward Lear's *Nonsense Songs and Stories*. 'Mr Yongy Bongy Bo', 'The Owl and the Pussy Cat' and the 'Old Man from the Kingdom of Tess', were favourites but then he enjoyed reading all of them. As I became more aware of the characteristics of local people and acquaintances he would ask me which of Lear's characters I was reminded of by certain persons. A stranger in the locality was referred to as an 'Akond of Swat'; if he had his hat pulled well down over his eyes he became a 'Quangle Wangle Quee' and an elderly couple who often called at tea time were privately known as 'The Owl and the Pussy Cat' for obvious reasons!

It was not until I recalled these bits of conversation that I realised how very private and personal to my father and myself were these allusions to other people, a sort of unspecified secret between us because it did not occur to either of us that it would be of any interest to my mother or my brother. There was no attempt to make a secret of it, though we were both aware that my mother was mildly contemptuous of such behaviour.

I had, and still have, a copy of Æsop's *Fables* illustrated by Arthur Rackham, and I don't mind confessing that I found some of the drawings rather awe-inspiring, particularly those of trees. One morning I was playing by the moat after an evening of reading Æsop when I chanced to look up and saw a most horrible 'face' in the bark of the willow tree in front of me. I rushed into the house where my parents were talking in the kitchen, grabbed my father round his legs and burst into tears. When he had pacified me he made me tell him what it was that had frightened me and after much sobbing I managed to make myself understood. My mother considered that it had been rather thoughtless to have shown me so many Rackham drawings but JC did not agree, saying that I had to get used to having an imagination and not to be frightened by it, 'After all he'll have to use it in the future.' Then he took me by the hand and made me lead him to the tree and show him the face, pointing out the eyes, nose and mouth with a stick which he gave me. After that I often saw 'faces' in the bark of willow trees but I wasn't frightened any longer. There was one tree, standing back from the water's edge, to which we became quite attached because the face was so cheerful and comic that one had to smile, though most of the faces had a dismal and woebegone aspect. However, as JC observed, who could be happy standing in water summer and winter.

JC's gift for creating confidence in other people, and in me in particular, did not always meet with my mother's approval and at times she was quite scathing. My father would listen, but rarely argue in front of me, but I got the impression that they talked things over after I had gone to bed. I recall one escapade of mine that caused quite a heated argument. My father had been telling me about sailing ships and reefing tops'ls in a gale. He had described how one had to forget everything else but the job, clutching at the straining canvas as one's body was thrown from side to side by the rolling of the ship and the confusion of the waves, first one side then the other, and how there was only your own physical strength and faith in God between you and a watery grave. I didn't realise at the time how dangerous it was. It didn't occur to me. It was just exciting, and I don't think I was being unduly silly or thoughtless when I tried to imitate the conditions which had excited me by climbing a very large oak tree that grew at the side of the north moat opposite the back door. It was a very tall oak, estimated at eighty feet to the top-most branches and I had been given, unwittingly, a way up by the provision of a swing from one of the lower branches, so it was not long before I learnt to climb one of the ropes and haul myself onto the bough, and from there it was relatively easy to climb right up to the top. I was quite happy. I wasn't scared and I enjoyed doing it but my mother did not like it at all. There were several heated arguments between her and my father for encouraging me to go up the tree. I arrived in the kitchen when one such argument was in progress and I tried to explain how my father had explained to me how to go up a mast in a gale of wind and I thought I'd like to do it as it seemed good fun, but I was 'shooed' out of the kitchen and the argument went on. After that JC always made a point of telling me not to discuss tree climbing in front of my mother but to wait until we were taking a walk round the garden.

3

Warping ships – stout ball of string – Hope –
maritime activities – visit to Hopes – vases – Hope's
quietness – sketching ships – no disparagement of
effort – ports and harbours – Strait of Malacca –
Otago and *Dragonfly* – JC falls into pond – newts and
fish – the lost swallow

As time passed my parents' anxiety for my safety round the moat
diminished and I spent many happy hours playing with my boats.
Occasionally in fine weather JC would come down to the waterside
and tell me how to berth them alongside the quay. Once JC was
helping me to warp a ship alongside when I only had cotton for use as
a rope and this kept breaking if pulled too hard. His patience soon
came to an end and after making her fast temporarily he said we
would tell the gardener to go down to Hamstreet to get a stout ball of
string. He called the man over and asked him to cycle down to the
village and get 'a stout ball of string'. The man looked a bit puzzled
and repeated 'A stout ball of string?'

'Yes. A stout ball and look sharp about it.'

He returned in about half an hour and handed my father a bobbin
of hop cord, about two feet long and six or seven inches in diameter.
JC looked at it and said, 'What the devil? I want string, strong string
not fine rope. Take the damned thing away and get some strong
string.'

'Yes, sir, very good sir, but you did ask for a "stout" ball, sir.'
There was a pause while they looked at each other and then they
both laughed. Sometime later my father told Captain Hope about
the 'stout' ball when he visited us and told him that at first he
thought the gardener was having him on but the man was quite
serious. For quite a long while afterwards, if I used a word in the
wrong place or sense, he would look at me and say, 'Stout ball, eh',
with a smile.

Captain Hope was the first of my father's friends of whom I really
took notice probably because of his interest in my 'maritime
activities'. Their friendship had commenced many years before my

arrival; but to me, at that time, it was because they were both captains, they both had beards and they both liked talking about the sea and ships. Captain Hope was not quite as tall as my father but, like JC he was always neat and tidy in his attire and his beard was just as well trimmed as my father's. He was a quiet and cheerful person who never, as far as I can remember, indulged in back-slapping or other boisterousness. His face was weather-beaten but not quite so heavily lined as my father's and he was always full of fun. He always wore a bright red waistcoat across which was slung a gold chain on the end of which he carried a gold repeater watch.

JC gave me a few days' notice when the Hopes were to pay us a visit so that I could prepare for his inspection which was usually made after they had had their after-lunch coffee. In my excitement I would forget to ask permission to get down from the table and would be called back and made to sit quite still for five minutes. Captain Hope would pull out his watch and set it to ring in exactly five minutes – it always seemed an awfully long time before the bell rang. After being told I could get down, I would rush to the side of the moat to see that all was ready.

After a while they would emerge from the house and stroll down to where I was waiting. They would want to know what the cargo was, where it came from and where it was consigned to. Then they would ask for the ships' papers! I was a bit disconcerted the first time they asked as I did not know what they were talking about. I hadn't any ships' papers but JC explained and after that I had small bundles of torn up newspapers for each of my ships. They would stand by the water's edge discussing my fleet, and I would hear 'I wouldn't like to be in a sea in that thing. Very poor freeboard' or 'A bit low in the fo'c'sle. Bury herself in anything but a dead calm.' At other times they would suggest improvements such as longer wharves, break-waters, dry docks, and more and better bollards. Then one day I was taken unawares by 'Who are the ships' chandlers?' I had no idea who or what chandlers were but JC came to the rescue and explained to Hope saying:

'New firm, Minnow, Stickleback and Tadpole, very well spoken of, very obliging, always send a man out as soon as you are sighted.' Hope burst out laughing and putting a hand on JC's shoulder he complimented him on his quick response, adding 'Now I know why they made you a captain.' After a while they would stroll away and I would hear snatches of conversation about people and ships they had known in the past but I was much too busy to listen!

During one summer we paid a visit to the Hopes at Fingeringhoe in Essex, crossing the river by the Gravesend Ferry. My mother anticipated that it was going to be a hot day and thought I would be cooler in a white shirt and white flannel shorts instead of my usual rig of blue jersey and serge shorts. That shirt was the most uncomfortable thing that had ever been invented quite apart from the fact that it was much too long for me. I fidgeted all the way over and when we arrived I insisted on being redressed to try and get more comfortable. The indignity of being publicly dressed didn't improve my temper. My father stood watching the proceedings and as soon as we were outside he said with a smile, 'Pull your shirt out of your bags and let it hang down outside, it will be cooler.' Having been brought up to be neat and tidy it never occurred to me that JC would approve, let alone suggest such a thing! Still, it was so hot he had taken off his own jacket!

While my mother sat and talked with Mrs Hope, the Captain took JC and me round the garden, from where we could see the lower reaches of the Thames, and eventually on to see his workshop. When Captain Hope had retired he had taken up making pottery as a hobby, throwing the vases and bowls on the potter's wheel, decorating them and firing them in his own kiln. We watched him make a little dish and then looked at the finished pieces which were displayed on shelves along the wall. He noticed my father looking at a pair of vases of very simple shape on which he had depicted junks sailing up an estuary with some palm trees growing on the banks. He took them down from the shelf and offered them to my father, asking him to accept them as a gift. JC looked at them closely for a short while and then thanking Hope for his offer said that he could not accept them. Hope was insistent and would not take no for an answer. JC picked them up and held them out to him asking him to look closely at the junks. 'The rigging is wrong, there is no steering oar at the stern, one junk appears to be sailing stern first as the mast is shewn forward of the lateen, and the reflections of the palm trees and the junks could not fall on the water between the junks and shore!' Hope took JC's criticism very well and asked if he could bring another pair, with the junks correctly rigged when he next came to visit us. For many years they stood on the mantelpiece in my room as a reminder of JC's remarks when he gave them into my care. 'You know the history of them. I could not take them knowing them to be wrong; it would have been damned hypocrisy. I'd have let the cat out of the bag and that would have upset Hope even more.'

To me the most remarkable thing about Captain Hope was his soft voice but I have no doubt that, had an occasion arisen, he could have produced a real quarter-deck shout. He spoke very clearly, each word carefully pronounced and complete in itself. I used to imagine them as little polished gems as they fell from his lips; it was extraordinary how peacefully he spoke. I know JC appreciated it because when the Hopes had left after a visit he would say, 'Dear fellow, he's so restful to talk to.'

Whether it was Hope's interest in my ships or JC's after-tea discourses with me (they were not lessons), I found I was taking far more care in making my harbours correctly and my ships more realistic. JC would 'cart me off' as he called it into the drawing room and with a matchstick dipped in ink draw sailing ships, naming the various parts as they took shape, but he never wrote in the names, so I had to remember them. I think this helped me to remember the names and certainly put an 'edge' on my attention while he was talking to me. He took me from the simple cutters to the full-rigged ship and whilst I remembered the various sails and parts of the hull I only remember scraps, and small scraps at that, of his recollections of his early life at sea. Nothing as far as I can recall that has not been included in his books.

At other times he would tell me about the Malay Archipelago and the Malays and show me pictures in A. R. Wallace's book about that part of the world. He would tell me about the villages built on piles along the sides of rivers and of how primitive bridges were built. At other times he described the purpose and the building of dams and irrigation canals and would spend whole evenings discussing water-wheels and their uses, and the operation of windmills.

My first attempts at building ships were pretty poor but JC was never disparaging about them, just observing 'It could do with a bit more freeboard' or 'What about putting a deckhouse about midships?' Sometimes I would get a bit of rigging wrong and be informed that 'The forestay should be made fast to the stem head, not aft of the fo'c'sle.' He never made a lot of suggestions at one time, which helped me to take in the information more easily. If I asked him some question about ships or shipping he always gave me a very full answer, but if I repeated a question to which he thought I ought to know the answer he would guide my thought so that I would find the answer myself.

At my father's suggestion I made a number of ports and harbours alongside of the moat. The first was 'Singapore' in the north-east corner where the ground sloped into the water at a very slight angle in the form of a shallow bay. It was very swampy at the edge which made digging the docks and building the wharves a fairly simple job. JC would come down and direct operations telling me where to put the twigs to mark the various areas. He was always most particular to see that the gardener or anyone else was not around on these occasions. If anyone appeared coming our way he would retreat from the water's edge telling me to take care and then stroll slowly away. If the person who had appeared went past us to the oast-house, JC would turn back as though he had remembered something he wanted to tell me. In reply to his questions at breakfast time I would tell him what I proposed doing but I never asked him to come and help so I never knew when he would appear.

A short distance from the north end of the moat a ditch ran in on the eastern side from another pond. This ditch rarely had water in it for more than about ten feet from the edge of the moat and, except in very wet weather, it was only the smallest ships that could navigate in it. JC helped me to build a little jetty with sticks and bits of a packing case and so the 'native village' of Patusan rose from the mud of a Kentish pond consisting of a shoe box, thatched with rushes, and the remains of the packing case precariously supported on sticks pushed into the bottom of the ditch.

From Patusan the bank ran south with pollarded willows growing at the water's edge and looking at their reflections through the months and years in a singularly inane way according to JC. Further along this side the high brick wall of the farmyard began and after about twenty feet or so a wall had been built at right angles across the south end of the sheet of water. This area was dubbed the Port of London, I suppose because of the brick walls. Westward from Singapore the bank across the north end was very steep to, and divided by, a large oak tree growing on the edge with its roots extending down some four feet to the water below, which JC likened to a miniature mangrove swamp. Going on up the side nearest the house there was just room to get by between the water and the bank at the side of the driveway leading round to the oast-house. Further on, some six feet above the water, on the edge of a fairly steep bank were three sheds and between the last two a very steep path down to the waterside. At the end of this path the ground had slipped away into the moat, leaving a channel about two feet wide which inevitably became the Strait of Malacca. From the end of the sheds the bank was unobstructed and sloped gently down to a fairly large bay, actually the eastern end of the southern part of the moat. There were quince trees along the edge with boughs stretching out over the water forming natural breakwaters and with a little 'engineering' by me with JC's' help we had the port of Bangkok on the Gulf of Siam, all of which could be seen from the drawing-room window.

I must have been a bit of a nuisance to the gardener as I was always pestering him to cut pieces of wood to the shape of a ship's deck, or to nail two pieces together to make a ship longer. After the hull had been shaped I would sit down on the floor of the wood lodge, find straight pieces for the masts, make up the fo'c'sle and poop, put on the deckhouse, and then set up the rigging after driving in rows of nails along gunnels. When it was finished to my satisfaction I would carry it down to the slipway at Bangkok, give it a shove and another ship was added to my fleet.

One of these I thought was a particularly good effort and was much the most realistic model that I had achieved. In fact I was so pleased with it that I set it up on the slipway again with the intention of asking JC to launch it after lunch. I was bubbling with excitement as we sat down to the meal and could hardly contain myself as my parents discussed various things. I knew better than to interrupt their conversation but at last JC turned to me and said, 'Well, what have you been up to this morning? You look very presentable, very neat, hair properly brushed and hands clean.'

'Dada, I have made a ship, a very good ship, which has a deck house, fo'c'sle and a poop and I want to call it *Otago*.'

He looked at me for a while then said, 'No. On no account are you to use that name for any of your pieces of wood. The *Otago* was a very fine and very fast little barque and I will not have her named dragged down to the level of a muddy pond.'

I apologised and tried to explain that as I had made such a good ship I thought I was being respectful to suggest naming it after a ship he had commanded. A rather crestfallen small boy finished his meal in silence and after asking permission to get down from the table went to JC and asked him to name and launch the new ship. A hug and a kiss and I was forgiven, and later that afternoon the ceremony took place. I am quite sure that my father had no idea what name to give the ship as he walked down to the slipway at Bangkok. The 'Gulf of Siam' always had a large number of dragonflies skimming over the water and so after looking at my preparations for the launch JC gave the ship a push and said very solemnly, 'I name this ship the *Dragonfly*. May she have a successful career.'

I had been given a yawl-rigged model yacht by a naval architect, Mr Hallowes, brother of Lilian Hallowes who later became my father's secretary. It was a most precious possession and I was only allowed to sail it when either JC or my brother could accompany me to the pond. Some days passed before we tried her out since long and animated discussions took place to decide on a suitable name for her. It was finally settled by my father that she should be called the *Narcissus* and she was named and launched from the new slipway at Bangkok which JC had helped me to build.

The moat was too weedy and the 'Round' pond near the north end was too small so we took her to a long but narrow sheet of water not quite half a mile away in the field opposite the 'Sugarloaf' cottage. It was about two hundred and twenty feet long by some thirty feet wide, with a spinney along the south side and a medium-sized oak tree stood on the edge of the high vertical bank at the eastern end where the water was quite deep. At the opposite end it was shallow for about four or five feet from the edge and JC always appointed me 'harbour master' here before taking up his position at the other end. On this particular day there was not a lot of wind and what there was was flukey but the *Narcissus* came steadily towards me. I caught her at the water's edge, turned her round, reset the sails and gave her a gentle push back to JC waiting at the other end. The wind dropped to the merest puff and the *Narcissus* barely moved but eventually she drew near the eastern end but then 'hove to' just out of JC's reach. After waiting a short while he hooked the walking stick he was carrying over a bough of the oak tree without realising it was rotten, and leant out over the water to grab the top of the mainmast. He had just reached it when, with a loud crack, the bough broke and JC fell into the deep end with a great splash. As the waves subsided I saw him slowly floundering towards the bank and rushed round to give him a hand as the water was over his shoulders. After much puffing and blowing he managed to get out and stand up with the water pouring from his clothes. I was much too concerned to laugh, which was as well, as he was very angry. He told me to pick up the yacht and we set off for home with JC muttering under his breath 'damned circus – blasted tree – fool enterprise'. By the time we reached the road he was in a better frame of mind and as we walked homewards he said,

'What an affair! I've been aloft furling the main tops'l in a full gale and survived and now to be nearly drowned in a muddy English pond would have been too bad but Fate relented. Keep all this to yourself. – Just say I slipped!'

The moat and the round pond were full of aquatic life, fish, newts, beetles and frogs, all of which I caught from time to time and kept in glass jars on the windows boards in the den. My father would come and look at them and occasionally help me change the water and put in fresh food. After about the fourth day of their captivity JC would suggest that I put them back into the pond and catch a fresh collection. At the time I thought it was a way of keeping me busy but I realised later that he had a great dislike of seeing any creatures kept in a confined space.

Early one morning in the autumn I found a young swallow which had been left behind when the rest of the swallows had migrated. It was perched on a rafter in the roof of one of the sheds and I managed to catch it and carry it into the house. With the help of Nellie Lyons we made a cage for it and after seeing that it was safely shut in I set about finding food for it, spiders, flies and any other insects I came across. It was not long before it sat on my finger while I carried it round the house looking for food. My father took a keen interest in the bird and would call me to come to the drawing room with the swallow to collect a daddy-long-legs or a fly. Some times it flew off and caught a fly on the wing, much to JC's delight, and then return to my finger to wait for any other food that might appear. I suppose we kept it for about three weeks before someone left the window open and it escaped. JC organised a search party and spent a long time with me looking in all the likely places, in the roof where I had found it first and in the loft of the oast-house. Some days later the gardener brought in the tiny corpse and JC, after looking at it, asked him to bury it.

On fine evenings I would go out after supper, about eight o'clock, to watch the owls and bats fly around, until nine when I was called to go to bed. I used to stand by an old pear tree on the far side of the kitchen garden opposite the back door and, if I had stood still enough, a large barn owl would alight at the top of the trunk where the branches started and sit there gazing round. In time it got used to me and I would feed it with a mouse taken earlier in the afternoon from one of my numerous cats. I told JC about my owl one dinner-time but he was not convinced, and asked me to pass him the salt. However after some persuasion he agreed to come with me one evening to wait for the owl. Several evenings passed before I managed to get it to take the mouse with JC standing beside me, but JC's pleasure at this achievement was somewhat spoiled when he realised that I had taken mice that the cats had caught, to feed 'this wretched bird'. On reflection it was strange how often he referred to an animal or a person as 'wretched' because in those days I do not recall hearing anyone else use the word to imply unimportance, which must have been the meaning that JC attributed to it. The owl looked anything but 'wretched' and was in very good condition. I remember hearing JC say when talking to my mother 'What a wretched affair' or 'what a wretched business'.

4

Dogs and cats – the postman – wasp sting – called
to drawing room – sennits – André Gide – meccano
– steam engines – kitchen table

My father was not particularly fond of dogs or cats so it always
mystified me how the dog knew that he was not allowed in the
drawing room or in my father's bedroom. I do not ever remember
seeing my father attempt to train the dog yet the animal seemed to
know and would not go into either room whether my father was there
or not. Appreciation of my father's wishes was not limited to Hadji,
the dog we had at Capel House, but also to his offspring Hadji-the-
Second, more often called Scallywag or Scally, who never crossed the
thresholds of my father's rooms when we lived at Oswalds.

Often when I was with my father in the drawing room the dog
would come and lie at the doorway to wait for me but he never came
into the room. Even the cats seemed to know that they were not
welcome but they did transgress occasionally when the dog chased
them. JC was always amused when I managed to get 'my tribe' to
follow me round the garden along the side of the moat nearest the
house. I would lead with Hadji immediately behind me, followed by
up to nine cats of various sizes and colours. These 'caravans' always
started by accident in the sense that I could never make the animals
follow me by order or cajolement. The dog kept close to heel when I
had my 'farmer's stick', a thin hazel wand about five feet long, as we
set out from the back door and turned right at the corner of the house
where the greater number of the cats joined us running out from the
sheds. Along past the side window of the drawing room and down to
the sumac tree where we turned right along the bank, collecting
other cats that were hunting along the line of the south moat, and so
on over the driveway by the west boundary hedge then turning east
and passing on to the driveway where it dipped before crossing the
north moat. I think the idea must have originated from a story in the

Mrs Conrad and John, Capel House

Boy's Own Paper as I was always given a bound volume of the previous twelve issues at Christmas. I am pretty sure that JC read it after I had gone to bed because I found little spills of cigarette ash between the pages. There were always one or two adventure stories, well written and exciting, with instalments spread over several months' issues. The language may have been 'superior' but at least one learnt how to speak.

Our regular postman always rode up to the front door to deliver the letters and made a point of patting Hadji and giving him a piece of biscuit when he ran out to meet him. One day a strange postman came. He left his bicycle by the little field gate at the roadside by the barn and walked across the field to the house. I was climbing in the sumac tree with the dog sitting nearby, catching twigs that I threw down to him. The postman walked past us, within a few feet, and up to the front door where JC was waiting. He ignored JC's 'Good afternoon' and walked back the way he had come, glaring at me and the dog as he passed. The dog watched him and then suddenly got up and went after him, took a firm hold of the seat of his trousers and pulled. By the time JC and I had recovered from our surprise the seat of the postman's trousers had been ripped neatly out and Hadji was trotting to the house proudly carrying the piece of blue cloth, which he deposited at JC's feet and then sat down beside him wagging his tail. The postman, rather embarrassed and very annoyed, returned to the house complaining bitterly and saying we ought not to keep such a savage beast. JC listened to his tale of woe and then called to Nellie Lyons to fetch a pair of flannel trousers from upstairs while he took the man through the house to the 'tween decks where he could change. JC explained to him how the other postman had behaved and told him that if he had taken a more friendly attitude the dog would not have torn his clothes. Then, giving him half a crown, sent him on his way. Next day the man came again, patted the dog, handed in the letters and a parcel containing the flannel trousers which JC told him to keep as they might be useful when he was gardening. Some months later he became our regular postman and turned out to be quite an amusing and cheerful character and my father would listen to his rather tall tales about the people he met on his rounds.

There is one day I shall never forget in the late summer when I was playing on the lawn outside the open window of the drawing room where my father worked. I was quietly rigging a ship in preparation for an official launching which JC had promised to perform later in the day. Suddenly I heard a 'quarter-deck' shout followed by far from subdued imprecations. Without waiting to see if I was the culprit I bolted for my hideout in the loft of the middle shed that stood beside the drive. I scrambled up the ladder closely followed by one of my pet cats, also suffering from fright, and there we stayed listening. There seemed to be much coming and going in the house and it was getting on towards lunchtime before I heard my name being called. I reluctantly left my refuge and went into the house to make myself tidy for, no matter what I had been doing, I had to be clean and tidy before I sat down to a meal. Everyone seemed rather subdued and even the gardener had no friendly word for me but went about his work muttering. Lunchtime came and I went to my place and sat down to wait, rather surprised that JC's chair was piled up with cushions. Presently he came in walking between two sticks and looking annoyed. I kept my eyes down waiting for the storm which I felt must break at any moment. He saw the cushions on his chair then looked at me but there was no smile on his face as he said,

'Well, what mischief have you been up to, you young scamp?' I denied having been up to any mischief and then my mother came in and asked JC how the sting felt. Seeing my look of surprise JC explained how he had sat on a wasp which had not respected him in the least and then went on to tell me that I should never assume responsibility for the action of others however small they might be. He tried to keep a straight face as he looked at me but I started to laugh and he joined me as he took the cushions and threw them into the corner of the room, remarking that he did not want all that 'damned fuss' just because of a wasp sting. My mother was really put out for JC had in fact made a lot of fuss before, calling for 'bluebag', onion and anything else that might alleviate the discomfort of the sting.

The orchard at Capel was a favourite place for wasps to build their nests and every summer there were quite a number of colonies. We would be at supper in the evening of a hot day with all the windows and doors open, when we would hear foot steps followed by a knock on the back door. Someone would answer it and we'd hear the deep voice of Mr Knight, who farmed the land round Capel House, saying: 'Would you tell the "maister" I be goin' t' take the "wopsies" nests. 'e might like t' come.'

JC always liked to accept these invitations and would call out, 'I'll be with you in a minute, presently.' He would ask me to fetch his cap and stick and we would go with Mr Knight to the orchard. During the day the old man would have marked the little holes of the entrances to the nests with twigs so that we did not have to search for them in the fading light. To 'take' the nest Mr Knight produced a length of gas pipe about three quarters of an inch bore and eighteen inches long with a cap on one end, with a small touch hole. This was filled with gunpowder and a length of fuse stuck into the touch hole. The open end of the pipe was pushed down into the nest and the fuse lit while everyone stood well away to one side and waited for the dull 'bumph' as the pipe was blown about four feet from the hole. Mr Knight then dug up the nest just to make 'sairtin' that all the occupants had been exterminated. It was a very efficient way of dealing with wasps and I do not remember anyone ever being stung on these expeditions.

One morning JC called me into the drawing room after breakfast. This was an unusual and vaguely worrying occurrence though I could not remember having done anything for which to be reprimanded so I tidied myself, pulled my jersey down, my stockings up and cautiously approached his desk. He was not writing but took no notice of me while he continued to fold a strip of paper into a kind of 'plat'. He put it on the blotter and pressed it down with his thumb nail before pushing it towards me. 'Do you know what that is?'

I knew better than to say a piece of paper so I was silent for a while and then said, 'A thing to put in a book to show where you are?'

He laughed saying, 'Yes. You could use it for that but it is called a sennit. If you were ship wrecked in the tropics you would collect wide grasses and after making a number of sennits you would fix them together to make a hat. Take it when you go and try to make one like it.'

Then, inviting me to sit on his knee he said, 'Now listen. Monsieur Gide is coming to lunch. I want you to be tidy, hands clean, hair brushed and waiting with me to receive him. He is a Frenchman so you will say "Bon jour, Monsieur. Comment allez-vous?" Now say that after me.' So for some minutes I repeated these words after JC though they did not mean anything to me. After a while JC asked me what was the matter.

'I don't know what the words mean.' You may well think this did not matter, but it mattered a great deal to me and other people because JC had the gift of making people do their best. He explained at some length, and after a few more repetitions by me I was allowed to go. What a long morning that was because as soon as I started doing something there was 'Mind you don't get dirty', or 'Leave the cat alone or you'll get covered in hairs.' Oh dear, everything was taboo so I went and sat on the window-seat in the dining room to wait. After a while I saw the taxi turn into the drive and jumped up to go and tell my father and in doing so butted him amidships as I had not heard him come and stand behind me. Monsieur Gide was a little surprised at JC's rather breathless greeting but I was forgiven as I did remember what to say.

After lunch, during which I was ticked off for giggling at the funny noises JC and Gide were making at one another I escaped to the den to play with my toys. Later in the afternoon I was very busy building something and was so intent on what I was doing that I did not notice them come into the room and remained so absorbed that they were on the point of leaving before I realised I was being spoken to – something about meccano. JC had shown me an advertisement some days before so I knew what it was. Gide was speaking to me but I didn't understand so JC explained that he was going to send me a box of meccano. I needed no coaxing to say 'Merci, monsieur' and spent the rest of the day in a happy dream about all the things I was going to build. It seemed an awfully long time before the set arrived – I was told later that I got quite annoyed with the postman for not bringing it.

I remember that JC was almost as excited as I was when it did arrive and we undid the parcel on the dining-room table. He spent most of the first evening helping me to build a simple model. He tried to put some of the parts together but his gouty fingers did not make it easy for him to handle the tiny nuts and bolts. I soon began to get the hang of things with his help and he would place an 'order' for a trolley or a cart and I would dash off and start building it without paying enough attention to the picture in the instruction book. I would get things a bit mixed up and JC would come and help me sort them out. As time went on I got better and his help was not so frequently needed. He encouraged me and whenever he went up to London he brought back an accessory set, going by taxi to Mr Lorberg's shop in Kensington High Street, before catching the train home.

I remember the first time he came home with an accessory set for me, as it caused a rift in the lute. He entered the house with a flat rectangular parcel under his arm, patted me on the head and kissed my mother as he usually did. He said something to her which I didn't catch and then in reply to something she said turned away from her saying, 'Well, I'm sorry Jess, I did not get anything for you. I'll make it right.'

A day or so later after he had been to Ashford I noticed my mother had on a new brooch and later on he gave me my first accessory set of meccano. After that he always gave my mother some trinket or piece of jewellery before giving me whatever he had got for me. He was most particular about getting the right accessory set so that my meccano set got progessively more complete. I think that Mr Lorberg must have kept a list of the sets that JC bought, so that he was able to hand him the right one as none was duplicated and each additional set enabled me to build larger and more intricate models. As soon as I had finished one I took it into JC's room and, if it was a model of a crane, I had to hold it down on the desk while JC operated it to lift a book from the floor. After the first time when the book fell from the hook he showed me how to make slings for lifting various objects and how to 'cord' a barrel to lift it 'upright' or horizontally. If he took a liking to a particular model it was just too bad because he wanted it left in his room so that he could have a good look at it. Still it was very rarely that he kept it for more than an evening.

As I became more proficient at building models some form of power was often needed so JC bought me various steam engines which between us we managed to adapt to drive the models. I use the word 'we' because he had a knack of spotting weakness in the design or arrangement of machinery and very often made suggestions for its improvement. His knowledge of steam engines was very extensive and he spent a long time operating the throttle valve and adjusting the timing while he explained how it worked and also improved its performance. If he went up to London after one of these sessions held in an atmosphere of steam, hot oil and metal, I could be pretty certain that he would return with an engine having even more refinements than the one I had. As my collection increased he insisted that I should be given a 'kitchen' table so that the spilt oil and water did not have to be constantly mopped up. This table was placed in the den and the various engines were screwed to it but I doubt if my mother was ever consulted about it or about the smell and noise in which she was expected to type my father's manuscripts. There were many occasions when I was told to put on my hat and coat and get out for a breath of fresh air, and to 'Open the windows before you go to blow the room clear.' The breath of fresh air usually meant climbing a tree or playing by the moat so it was no real hardship.

5

Tree climbing – look out for guests – shopping –
gardening – pedal motor – reward for careful
driving – silent travel – horn – ashtray –
oast-house – hops – sulphur up –
pressing – pocketing

With so many trees around, my father realised that I was bound to
climb them so he gave me instructions on how to 'hang on'. My
mother did not approve and often asked him not to encourage me but
she did not press her objections. My father's attitude was that it was
better to give me instruction on how to take care of myself rather than
deny me this form of activity which he thought would help to make
me more self-reliant. After a time my tree climbing was accepted by
my mother but, by tacit understanding between my father and
myself, it was not discussed when my mother was present. JC always
seemed to know when I wanted to tell him about an attempt to climb
a particular tree and would propose a walk round the garden. Then
he would often suggest a better route up a tree or an easier way round
a bough.

When a guest was coming he would send me up a tree at the end of
the drive which we called the 'foremast'. I would climb up into the
topmost branches, right up into the 'crow's nest' from where I could
see the main road about half a mile away. As soon as I saw a car
approaching I would give JC a hail, and then wait until I saw it turn
into the lane by the 'Sugarloaf'. I usually managed to get down the
tree and into the house by the time it arrived at the door. The lane
was surfaced with crushed flints, sharp as razors, which were the
principle cause of the numerous punctures we had in those days.
Most drivers drove very slowly over them but whether that reduced
the number of punctures is debatable. Most of the lanes were
finished with this flint as well as some of the, so-called, main roads
and it stood up well to the iron-rimmed wheels of the horse traps and
waggons as well as providing a good grip for the horses' hooves.

Our only means of transport when we went to Capel House was a pony and trap and nearly every day the pony was harnessed for a journey somewhere, either into Ashford or down to Hamstreet, where we did most of our shopping. In those days the 'Duke's Head' stood right on the edge of the road with the stable-yard behind and it was there that we tied up the pony while we shopped. My mother made her slow and painful way along to the shops which were all within about two hundred yards of the Inn. First we went to Mrs Godden's, the farthest away, for newspapers and sweets, then to the bakers for flour, the greengrocers, and then the post office on the way back. The seemingly leisurely existence of those days has gone, likewise the friendly greeting from the shopkeepers who always produced a chair or stool for my mother to rest on while she gave her orders. In the summer there was an extra port of call at Mr Malam's farm for cherries, one of JC's favourite fruits, though the fruit he preferred above all others were raspberries.

We grew nearly all our own vegetables but my father was no gardener in any sense of the word and my mother could not do anything on account of her damaged knee, so the ordering of seeds and the growing of plants was left to the gardener or rather a succession of gardeners. Some took advantage of the apparent lack of interest and stocked up their own gardens as well as over-ordering for our needs; their employment terminated with a lecture on honesty by JC and payment of what was due to them.

I remember my father's annoyance when he saw a large sack of surplus vegetables being taken away and his demand to know why he should be called upon to provide 'half the village with vegetables?' The storm abated somewhat when he learnt that they were going to the local hospital as a gift. I think that the almost continuous pain that my mother suffered was the cause of occasional injudicious remarks at these times when she suggested that he should do the ordering and planting of the seeds. JC however would make it abundantly clear that he had no intention of doing anything of the kind. It was only very rarely that he picked a flower and never pulled a weed though he liked well-arranged flowers in the house and expected vegetables to be provided in season. It always surprised me that his favourite flower should be mignonette, though if he bought flowers for my mother, they were roses or carnations unless she had asked for something else.

One day in each week Mr Spicer, the carrier, called on his way to Ashford to pick up the list of goods which we wanted him to bring us on his return. On one particular day he arrived back just before tea and, as I had had a number of presents for my fifth birthday, I was rather surprised to be called in and told to go to my father who was standing by a box-like parcel in the den. I did not appreciate what it was until we started to remove the wrappings. There must have been squeals of delight when it dawned on me that it was a pedal motor, so heavy and solid but not so primitive that one could not tell what it was supposed to be. It was painted green with red coach lines round each panel but there were no doors. It had a wooden steering-wheel, several imitation dials on the dash board and a padded seat of quite exceptional firmness. There were no springs, the axle-mountings were bolted direct to the chassis and there were four large pram-wheels with solid tyres between me and the ground. An uncased chain took the drive from the pedals to the back axle and when this had been oiled so were my stockings. When all the wrappings and string had been removed I gave JC a 'thank-you' hug and clambered in and just managed to make it move. Suddenly my father left the room but returned in a very short while carrying a bottle of olive oil with which he lubricated the bearings. It was not long before I was all over the house knocking off large flakes of paint here and there. It was not an ideal house for a pedal car as there was a massive oak threshold at each doorway some four inches high which necessitated getting out of the car, lifting first the front and then the rear wheels over the obstruction.

After numerous injunctions to be careful not to bang the paint-work my father offered me threepence for every trip I made from the den to the drawing room without hitting the paintwork. How my driving improved! The scale of reward had to be revised in a very short time as JC could not get enough threepenny bits to keep up to date. In all but the heaviest rain I would be out in the car rushing from the oast-house to the lane at the end of the drive, making 'exhaust' noises through my lips. This was very tiring when one had to make the noise, provide the power and breathe so I was very grateful to the gardener when he showed me how to fix a straightened hairpin to the chassis so that the other end caught on the spokes of the back wheel. It made a much better noise as far as I was concerned but it was not long before I was told to stop 'that damned racket'. JC gave me a long talk on the advantages of silent travel like a steam car. Mechanical noise was an indication of inefficiency and the noisier a vehicle was the more inefficient it was and 'of course you do not want people to think your car is inefficient'. In the end we came to a compromise and I was allowed to use my 'clicker-clacker' either where JC could not hear it or when he was away. My mother did not like the noise but I do not remember being told by her to stop it.

I took my father's talk on efficiency a bit too literally one day when he was sitting under the sumac tree. I managed to drive close up behind his chair over the grass without being heard and got a severe dressing-down for making him jump, I explained that I was trying to be efficient and apologised for giving him a shock. He forgave me, and the next time he went to Ashford, bought me a horn for the car. That was a mistake – in half an hour I was forbidden to use it except at blind corners, real ones not imagined, or if anyone meandered about in my way. I was never to use it in the house. Some time after my fifth birthday my mother suggested that I should give my father a present, not on his birthday but around that time to show my gratitude for being given the pedal motor. JC did not like the family to remember his birthday and it was not made the occasion for a celebration of any kind. My mother usually gave him a present around this time of the year but I never heard her wish him 'Many happy returns of the day' and when he gave a present he never used the traditional phrase but would say, 'Here is a present, I hope it's what you want.' He always remembered my mother's birthday, those of my brother and myself and those of any young friends.

It was left to me to decide what I should give him and a chance remark by him provided the answer when he wanted to know. 'Who is the damned fool who has taken away the saucer from my bedside that I use as an ashtray?' For some reason the job of buying an ashtray was delegated to Mr Spicer, the carrier, probably because I had a cold, though I clearly remember standing in the back hall by the door to wait for him. He used to drive round to the back door and get down off his cart to take the order while his horse pulled the cart to the corner, where there was more room, turned the cart round and returned to the door to wait for him and be given an apple. I had to wait patiently while the order was written down before asking him: 'Please, will you get a threepence "smooth at the top" ashtray?' He wrote it down carefully, took my three pennies and promised to bring it on his return. I am sure that the simple copper and brass ashtray cost more than I gave him and that my mother must have made up the difference. After tea my father offered to read to me. Clutching a book in one hand and the ashtray, neatly wrapped up, in the other, I presented myself at the side of his chair. I handed him the parcel, saying it was for him because he had given me the pedal motor. I was a little surprised when he put it on the table, lifted me onto his knee, then picked it up and gave it to me to open for him. From that day for the rest of his life that ashtray was always on his bedside table and very definite instructions were given that it was to be emptied and dusted but never polished with metal polish; these instructions have been observed and ever since his death it has been on my bedside table, one of my most treasured possessions.

While we lived at Capel the oast-house was used for drying hops which grew in the fields nearby. Mr Knight, the farmer, took up his 'residence' as soon as picking started and would be round about the oast continuously while the hops were being dried. The Capel oast has a single kiln, at the eastern end of a barnlike building, some sixteen feet in diameter with a narrow passage round the inside giving access to the four fire holes. These are formed in the brickwork of the inner side of the passage which rises about five feet vertically before starting to slope outwards to meet the outer wall of the kiln at about twelve feet above the floor. At the point where they meet is the drying floor consisting of stout beams on which are fixed battens about two inches square at four inch centres. Each year this floor was always carefully overhauled and any doubtful timbers replaced before new coarse canvas netting of about quarter of an inch mesh was stretched and fixed down. It was on this mesh that the hops were spread for drying by the heat from the fires below. Some four feet above the drying floor the roof sloped cone-wise and terminated in a round hole over which a wooden cowl was mounted on a spindle which allowed it to rotate. An arm about five feet long stuck out from an opening in the side of the cowl which had to be kept to leeward so as to draw the smoke and fumes out of the kiln. From the first floor of the main building there was a short ladder leading up to the drying floor through a wide doorway which had three or four deep 'stall' boards across it. These were removed when the hops had been dried so that they could be shovelled out of the kiln onto the 'press' floor ready for pocketing.

My father always took an interest in hop drying though he was not a beer drinker and it was very seldom that he had any since he preferred a whisky and soda. I would go with him to the oast-house in the evening to see how the work was progressing and stay for a chat with Mr Knight to whom we would take a bottle of beer, a twist of ''baccar' and a pocketful of chestnuts if we remembered. We tossed these in to the edge of the fire and when they had been roasted we hooked them out and ate them. If we were there around nine in the evening Mr Knight would be having some refreshment and JC would have a mug of 'cold tea' – a dark mahogany coloured liquid, very sweet, and I suspect liberally laced with rum because I was never allowed to have more than a tiny sip.

Mr Knight made himself very comfortable with a heap of old hop sacks to lie on, spread along a rough wooden bench near the entrance to the 'fire' walk. The fires needed attention every three or four hours day and night so to keep him aware of his duty he had an immense and incredibly noisy alarm clock, with a tick like a hammer on an oil drum. It always amused me to see him put it under a pile of sacks when my father arrived as though it was something indecent but it was so noisy that it made conversation quite difficult.

When Mr Knight was feeling particularly friendly or may be when he was tired he gave each of us a stick of sulphur and asked us to help him 'sulphur up' by putting a piece about an inch long into the fires. This was a slow job as each piece has to be consumed before the next piece was thrown in so that the hops had a 'proper doing'. When this had been done to his satisfaction we would be invited to go up to the drying floor to watch him turn the hops. This was done with a spade-shaped affair made up with battens and covered with a fine canvas, about two feet wide and eighteen inches long with a handle about three feet long.

On one occasion JC offered to help turn the hops and Mr Knight thanked him but warned him that 'the sulphur doan' ''arf ketch yew if yew're no us't to it'. JC said that he could probably put up with it as he had no doubt smelt worse. I watched the two men ascend the short ladder up to the drying floor and step over the stall boards, their shadows made enormous by the light of the lantern hanging by the side of the door. They started to turn the hops which usually took Mr Knight about ten to fifteen minutes, but JC only spent about two to three minutes in the hot sulphurous air before clambering out gasping for breath. As soon as my father had recovered we took our leave of the old man, who acknowledged our 'Good night' without looking up or stopping his steady rhythmic swing as he turned the hops. As we returned to the house JC remarked that it was much too much like Hades, with the heat and sulphur fumes and the grotesque shadows wheeling across the inside of the kiln. 'How does the old man stand it? He certainly ought to go to Heaven.'

After the hops had been dried they were pressed into a long sack, called a pocket, about eight feet long and thirty inches in diameter. The pressing usually took place in the morning and JC would often come with me to see how things were going. Mr Knight and I often had disagreements over the proper use of haystacks as I used to annoy him by sliding down the slopes which formed when the stack was cut. He was a friendly person and used to try to mystify me by saying he was going to 'drop a sack and hang it', and the first time he said it neither JC nor I knew what he was talking about. The 'pockets' were stacked and neatly rolled up so that Mr Knight could take the 'open' end and drop the rest of the sack through the hole in the floor under the press. Then, kneeling on the floor, he rolled the open end round an iron ring which was then wedged in position round the hole. Thus his mysterious remark was explained.

Over the hole there was a simple framework carrying a toothed bar with a circular pad on the end which would just pass through the hole. The toothed bar engaged with a cogwheel on the driven shaft at the end of which was a large cog engaging with a small cog attached to another large cog which in turn engaged with a small cog of the first shaft. Also on the first shaft was a rachet wheel with which a pawl engaged and the ends of this shaft were made square so that handles could be fitted onto them. To begin with the pocket was filled about two thirds full of dried hops, the pawl was released and the pad descended compressing the hops by its weight. The handles were fitted to the ends of the first shaft, the pawl was engaged and the real pressing then started, with my father and Mr Knight heaving and pulling at the handles until they would go no further. While the pressure was held by the pawl Mr Knight got a fresh batch of hops ready for shovelling in. At a word from Mr Knight pressure was put on a handle and the pawl released and the pad wound up clear of the top of the pocket. Then more hops were shovelled in and the handles wound round to press each batch of hops and so on until the pocket was full. A sling was then tightened under the pocket to take the weight while Mr Knight sat on the floor to sew up the end. He put a sail-maker's palm on his hand and took up a long curved needle which he threaded with a stout line and began the job of closing the pocket. He took great pride in finishing it 'proper like', starting with a corner 'taken up to an ear' then rolling the edges and overstitching them to the other corner which was also finished with 'an ear'.

My father used to watch him and on one occasion said, 'I wish I had had you as sail maker when I was at sea.'

Mr Knight looked up at him to see if he was joking but realising that JC was serious took the clay pipe from his mouth and said, 'I doan think yew 'ould. The sea and me doan agree, I'd a bin mortal sick I sh'ud.' JC was careful not to show his amusement at the vehemence of Knight's reply and for a while afterwards used words 'doan agree' though never in Knight's hearing.

6

Cadillac – Gibbons at Dymchurch – Marsh fog –
half men and cows – lost wheel – calmness
at the unexpected – Campbell and Leacon Hall
corner – Model T Ford – waggon and horses –
Gibbons at Trottiscliffe

Early in 1912 my father bought our first car, a single-cylinder chain-driven two-seater Cadillac with two forward speeds and reverse. Before its arrival we used to hire a car from one of several firms in the district but mostly from Haywards of Ashford who, I believe, carried out the modifications to the Cadillac that were needed to accommodate the family. It had no running-boards or doors but there was a hood which when erected kept off most of the rain. When the car first arrived there was only a narrow step, just wide enough for one foot, which made it very awkward for my mother to get up to the passenger seat, so running-boards were fitted. A part of the nearside one was made to lift up so the starting handle could be pushed onto the crankshaft, just aft of the passenger's seat.

The driving seat off a horse drawn 'wagonette' was acquired and fixed over the engine cover high enough for the occupants to see over the hood when it was folded back. It served very well as a 'dickey' seat though it was not very comfortable and decidedly chilly in any but the hottest weather. It had a back consisting of a horse-hair padded board, similar to the seat with small iron-rod armrests each side, which were very necessary for me as I often had to hang on to prevent myself from being flung overboard at corners.

My father did learn to drive but he was not a sympathetic driver and treated the car like a pony and trap. If it slowed down on a hill he would mutter, 'Come on, come on. You can manage' and did not change down until the car had almost come to a standstill. When my brother was at home he always drove and at other times the chauffeur–gardener would take the wheel. In the summer we would run down to Dymchurch where Percival Gibbon had rented a house for his family holiday. We arrived soon after lunch and stayed on for an evening meal prepared by Maisie Gibbon and my mother, ignoring the possibility of a mist forming over the marsh. My mother sat in front beside the driver and JC and I would clamber up and perch on the dickey seat wrapped in a waterproof rug (a relic of the horse-and-trap days) when it was raining or foggy.

On clear nights JC would point out the various star formations, the Plough, the Bear and Pole star and describe how the mariners used them to determine their position at sea. Fairly often a marsh mist would form, rising about two to three feet above the ground and hiding the road from the driver's view yet leaving the dickey seat passengers' heads in clear air looking out over a white blanket. With deep dykes each side of the road and only the grass verge to steer by, progress was very slow and if there was a moon it was even slower. My father and I sitting up on the dickey would see the upper half of a house or a haystack slowly approach us, like some animal stalking its prey, slowly rotate and disappear. A line of trees without trunks or roots would materialise, swing round and vanish. An owl would rise from the sea of mist, fly past in silence and vanish like some phantom from another world. Then we would hear above the noise of our passage the fitful dirge of a lost soul. We would meet a horse and cart without lights with the driver, more often than not, very drunk and signing gustily to keep the 'spirits' at bay while the horse found its own way home. In those days the roads were very narrow and when two vehicles met they had to pass one another with two wheels on the grass verge. There were no protective railings or signs to warn one of bends and junctions and even today the marsh is no place to be if there is a fog and a bright moon. My father often remarked that he would sooner sail up an eastern river without leading marks than try to find his way along the 'snake back' roads of Romney Marsh in a fog.

Recalling the marsh fogs I am reminded of autumn evenings at Capel when my father would accompany me to the fence along the north side of the garden beyond the end of the moat where a thick mist about eighteen inches high formed over the fields. The soil all round was heavy clay, and water could not get away, so we would often see the strange sight of the upper part of a woodman's body returning home from work accompanied by a rhythmical sloshing noise as he went by. It was even stranger to see cows without legs moving around making weird noises, suckings and gurglings, squelches and bubblings, and if they were moving when it was dark it was even more eerie. My mother and Nellie Lyons were not taken in by our remarks about the 'half-men' and ghosts and, apart from telling us not to get our feet wet, took no interest in our escapade.

Living on the fringe of Romney Marsh, which was an important sheep breeding area, we often encountered large flocks of sheep being either driven to or from Ashford Market. On one such day JC was sitting in front beside the chauffeur, while I was alone on the dickey seat, and as we approached the left hand bend, just before Shipley Hatch Cross, a flock of sheep came into sight. We started to slow down and were somewhat surprised to see a wheel and tyre rolling away ahead of us into the sheep. As the car came to a halt there was the crunch of metal as the axle hit the road while the shepherd came towards us carrying the wheel. He came up to my father and looking him in the face said, very seriously: 'Your wheel I believe sir.' JC glared at him and said, 'Of course it is, damned fool. Thank you.' We got out of the car and I was dispatched after the shepherd, who had gone after his sheep, to apologise and give him a tip.

Albert Bampton (coachman–chauffeur) and John, Capel House

This minor mishap seemed to upset JC far more than more serious accidents; perhaps it was annoyance more than fright that made him react as he did. Even at that age, five or six, I was aware of his calmness in the face of the unexpected and how, when the emergency was over, he did not 'harp back' to the event. It was over and done with and passed into history – why waste time arguing about it? If there was anything to be gained in raking over the ashes he was ready to discuss it providing there were sufficient facts to do so.

A friendship had developed with a Doctor Kenneth Campbell of Wittersham, who became a regular visitor, as he was an amusing and cheerful person and got on well with my parents. He was a keen motorist and often took my mother for a drive along the lanes before going home. He turned up one day in a new Calcot two-seater just before lunch and JC insisted on making an inspection before we sat down to the meal. Campbell praised the car's road-holding ability, instancing a corner at Warehorne which he had taken at thirty miles an hour. After some conversation JC said that the Cadillac could probably do as well. Campbell disagreed, it was too high and rather top heavy and, with respect, not powerful enough to reach thirty miles an hour. JC observed that one could try and see if it was possible, but Campbell said that the Cadillac was not the sort of car to experiment with though he would not try to dissuade JC. The subject was changed and no more was said on either side.

At the time I did not notice any rift between the two men but I think that JC must have been a little put out by the implication because a few days later he told Albert Bampton, our chauffeur, to bring the car to the door as he wanted to go for a run. As it was then mid-morning we were all rather surprised at this and I hung around the back door to see what was going to happen. JC was ready in his heavy havelock coat and bowler hat and getting into the driving seat, when he saw me standing by the old car. He looked at me again and said, 'Come on. Scramble up.' I was up on the dickey seat almost before he had finished speaking, up on the 'poop', and tense with excitement.

As soon as we moved off I was aware of an urgency in our progress; JC was driving with great verve and confidence. We rushed down the drive and out onto the road – luckily nothing was coming – and on along the lane to the main road. The old car seemed to respond and the thud of the single cylinder below my feet sounded crisper than usual. The speed rose as we descended the hill into Hamstreet. We slowed down for the corner with a series of deafening back fires, round by the post office, missing a horse and cart by fractions of an inch, and charged away through the arch under the railway and pounded up the hill towards Warehorne. As we approached the corner by Leacon Hall at considerable speed I heard JC shout above the noise of the wind, 'Hang on aft! We're going about', and 'about' we went, right round on two wheels and into the field gate. After the crash of broken timber there was silence, so complete that I almost jumped when a lark started to sing overhead. As I watched a little column of steam rise from the radiator I became aware of JC looking at me, 'So you stayed aboard then?' then he looked at Bampton who was rather white and said, 'You take over. Restore your confidence. I knew she'd do it but I did not expect her to go right about. Don't mention this to anyone. I have just proved a point, that's all.'

We returned home at a very sedate pace taking all corners at a very low speed. The experiment was not repeated which was as well and I do not think that my father ever realised that he had taken the corner from the wrong direction which made it far more difficult. It was many years later that I realised this, but my father had approached the corner from the east, Hamstreet side, whereas Dr Campbell coming from Wittersham would have approached it from the west, through Appledore Heath and Kenardington. Even coming from the west it required a good car and above average skill to take this corner at more than twenty-five miles an hour, even if the road was clear and full use could be made of the width.

I assume it was one Sunday morning, for the chauffeur was not about, that my father called me to go with him to start the car which was kept in a lean-to garage on the end of the oast-house. After going through the usual drill of checking tyres, water and oil, the running-board was hinged back and the large starting handle was pushed onto the end of the crankshaft. The petrol was turned on, the carburettor 'tickled' and the engine turned over several times. Then on a signal from JC I turned the switch and he cranked the engine over and, usually, it started. In those days it was the practice to let the engine warm up, so, having set the throttle, we returned to the house for our hats and coats. Perhaps we were a bit longer than usual before we emerged and started back to the oast-house. As we approached all we could see was a cloud of dust rising from the open doorway. We hurried to the shed where we could hear the engine

Joseph Conrad wearing his havelock coat. Mrs Conrad and John, outside Capel House

chugging away and when we looked inside we could just discern the outlines of the car through the dust. We had forgotten to apply the handbrake and the single-cylinder engine placed lengthwise in the chassis had caused the car to oscillate to and fro with the result that it had knocked a large hole through the rear of the shed. Having satisfied himself that the car was all right, JC drove it out followed by more dust and broken bricks. He waved to me to get aboard and with a few pithy remarks about the incompetence of builders drove away leaving a trail of bricks and dust to mark our passage.

Some time later we parted with the Cadillac and became the owners of a Model T Ford, which also had an enormous windscreen, but it was much more lightly built. Many people agree that though a car is manufactured it does have a character of its own, though whether it acquires it from the men who built it or from the first or subsequent owners is a debatable point. This particular Ford must have had an unhappy start to life; it was vicious and often 'took charge' if one got too near the side of the road. The coils for the ignition, one for each cylinder, were mounted on the dash just above the driver's left foot. One of these became loose on our first trip and gave the driver a severe shock through his damp shoe but luckily for us his reaction was quick, otherwise it could have been our last journey.

The Ford was not a wise choice with its foot operated gears and unpredictable behaviour on the road. On several occasions when JC was driving he managed to get mixed up as to which pedal was the brake and which the reverse. On more than one occasion we would come to an abrupt halt and start going backwards which was exciting and not a little disturbing, though not very dangerous as there was not much traffic about, mostly waggons and horses or an occasional trap. Writing of waggons reminds me of the day we emerged from the drive at Capel to find our way blocked by a hay-waggon drawn by two large cart-horses. We managed to stop as the carter came out from the cottage at the end of the drive where he had been talking with the occupant. The sudden stop had also stopped the engine of the Ford so my father leant over the side and called to the man to 'Give her swing.' He made two attempts and on the third there was a terrific bang as the silencer burst and, before the noise had died away, the waggon was gathering speed as the horses bolted. Even from behind it was a frightening sight to see the waggon with four or five tons of hay aboard go swaying down the lane but the weight soon tired the animals and they came to a standstill before they reached the main road.

We often went for an afternoon drive when my brother was at home. My mother sat beside him and JC and I occupied the back seats. Before very long my father would want a cigarette. He would put one in his mouth and take one match and try to light it, then two matches, then three matches, without success. Then he took about half a dozen matches, arranged them in echelon close together and struck the first one in the hope that the cigarette would be lit by the time the last one flared up, but even this failed. He would take the cigarette out of his mouth, look at it, throw it overboard, take the packet from his pocket, look at it, throw it overboard, then a few seconds later the matchbox as well. We would travel on in silence for a while and then he would lean forward and touch my brother on the shoulder and ask him to stop at the next tobacconist.

At about this time the Gibbons had gone to live near Wrotham Heath at Trottiscliffe on the south side of the North Downs about thirty-two or three miles from Capel House. We now had a Humber touring car and we would climb into it and arrive at Trottiscliffe about four o'clock. I played with the two girls, Joan and Joyce, until their bedtime when I would be given a book to look at until my parents decided to return home. This was nearly always after an evening meal but on one particular evening it was nearly eleven before we set off. We passed through Charing at about midnight and turned onto the Ashford road. After climbing a slight rise, the engine faded and we rolled to a standstill within sight of the Olive Branch Inn. All was quiet under a bright moon, mist was rising from the fields on each side as the chauffeur got down to have a look under the bonnet. After a short while he found that the drive to the magneto had sheared and that a temporary repair was not possible. My father decided to try to telephone Haywards in Ashford to send a car to take us home. He set off to walk to the inn where we heard him knocking on the door, each time more insistently than before, but there was no reply. We sat and waited. I began to feel cold so my mother made me take off my shoes and put my feet behind her along the back of the seat while she tucked the rug round me. After what seemed an age we heard my father approaching and, as he sat down in the front seat, he explained that he had gone on to a farm where he had seen a light and had managed to get through to Haywards. He sat there whistling and shrugging his shoulders as he did when he was annoyed. After a while he turned to my mother and said, 'Jessie, those people will want more than an olive branch next time.'

Another long wait and then a rumbling in the distance heralded the arrival of a large 40 horse-power Fiat. A tow rope was produced and our car hitched on and we proceeded sedately to the garage where we left the Humber to be repaired and then went on home. Soon after this we parted with the Humber as it always seemed to break down in the grand manner and require new parts. I believe that its successor was a Studebaker, much more up to date with an electric starter and lights, and a proper hood with side curtains which really kept out the rain.

7

Garnett – Millais – Symons – Will Cadby –
Douglas – Oliver – Hueffeur – Cunninghame
Graham – Marwood – Horton Priory and
Jenny – Galsworthy – Richard Curle

My father expected me to be in attendance when guests arrived or departed when I was at home, and I had to be presentable and as neat and tidy as he was. He never failed to remind me if I was slack and untidy in my dress that it gave a bad impression, and that being neat and tidy in appearance gave people confidence in you as it showed that you had a correct attitude to life. In the same way one should be 'courteous, it costs nothing but discourtesy can ruin you'.

When we had a car of our own it was my duty to meet our friends at the station, acting as deputy for my father, and when they left I had to accompany them to the railway station to see that they were taken to the correct side for the London train. I used to enjoy doing these commissions for my father, and I think other people did as well. Somehow one felt it was a privilege to do things for him.

As far as I can remember Edward Garnett was the first person I was sent to meet and, although he was a fairly frequent visitor, I always had the feeling that he treated my father with a slight amount of reserve; but maybe I was wrong and it was simply respect. There is no doubt Uncle Edward enjoyed coming to see us as much as JC enjoyed his visits, for the mental stimulus that they provided and for the opportunity of hearing his opinions, though not always agreeing with them. When I was old enough Uncle Edward got me to take him for rambles in the woods around Capel. We would start with a tour round the moat and then strike off across the fields and into the woods. After walking in silence for a while he would break it by quoting from Edward Lear, usually from the 'Courtship of the Yongy Bongy Bo':

> On the coast of Coromandel
> Where the early pumpkins blow,
> In the middle of the woods
> Lived the Yongy Bongy Bo.

I would finish the verse:

> Two old chairs, and half a candle, –
> One old jug without a handle, –
> These were all the worldly goods;
> In the middle of the woods, etc etc

Edward Garnett

I remember walking in the woods to the east of Capel when we came across a woodman cutting the chestnut undergrowth: the Yongy Bongy Bo, a bit further on where he had made a fire to boil the water for his tea we came across 'Two old chairs and half a candle, one old jug without a handle ...' The 'two old chairs' was a bit far-fetched as they were two rough piles of logs but the candle was there and was obviously used to start the fire. Uncle Edward commented on the aptness of the verse and regretted that we had not found the 'Lady Jingly Jones'. He need not have worried as round the next bend in the path we came upon a woman, the woodman's wife, but she did not come up to Lear's illustration of Lady Jingly Jones. We told JC of our encounter when we got home and Garnett tried to get him to agree to come with us for a walk next day but he would not commit himself.

JC's gift of being able to 'get alongside' people made him an easy person to talk to as he always listened to what was said with attention. He had the most disconcerting ability of detecting a lie or any 'fabrication of doubtful facts', and he had no time for hypocrisy or conceit. Garnett was a very genuine person and so got on well with JC and with the rest of the family but he was primarily JC's friend. I do not remember Constance Garnett ever coming to stay with her husband though I believe she did come once or twice before I was old enough to take notice.

I got on well with Garnett. He was a serious person with a kindly disposition, a friendly face with deep creases down to each corner of his mouth which gave him a vaguely 'froglike' expression. This did not occur to me until one day when he arrived with a string bag of vegetables, of his own growing, as a gift for my mother. After she had welcomed him my father 'carted him off' to his room while I followed my mother back to the kitchen carrying the string bag. My aunt was staying at the time and as my mother entered the kitchen she said, 'As you see, Jeremy Fisher has arrived.' I was amused at this reference to the Beatrix Potter character but I soon reverted to 'Uncle Edward' as being much more appropriate. I was really fond of him, not because he gave me money when I escorted him to the station; no, his trick of quoting Lear helped to form a particular kind of friendship. He took notice of me and listened to my childish chatter as though it was of importance and this helped to build up my trust in him.

He was about the same build as my father but somehow lacked the presence that JC had and did not give the impression of being a leader of men as my father did. In a gathering of people one was aware of an 'observer', shrewd and kindly but not immediately obvious and, when he was the only guest, one felt there was a benign 'shadow' present. Although he was slow of speech he was a compelling speaker, enunciating the syllables clearly without wasting words, yet conveying his thoughts precisely. I was always struck by the peacefulness of his conversation, he rarely raised his voice or betrayed any excitement, yet at the same time he retained the attention of his listeners.

He was sombrely dressed in a dark suit, grey shirt, a plain subdued tie and black boots. The suit appeared rumpled, the waistcoat liberally dusted with the ash from his herbal cigarettes which he never succeeded in persuading my father to smoke. Privately JC referred to them as damned vegetables. His face lacked colour, and his dark eyes and dark-grey unruly hair gave him the appearance of a rugged untidiness which did not seem to be in keeping with his nature.

When we were tramping through the woods conversation came in bursts but I was never aware of any effort on his part to bring the level of conversation down to that of a person of my age. Not that our conversation was very edifying, being mostly concerned with natural history though occasionally we would speculate on a lunch-time guest or on the people we met in the fields and woods. Once we stopped to watch an old farmhand layering a hedge and it was some time before he became aware of us. When he did, he laid down his billhook and stood with his hands on his hips gazing at us in silence but as we prepared to move on he found his voice:

'You'm an old'un t'hev such a yung'un.' Then he realised who the 'yung'un' was.

'Sorry guv'ner, did'nt rekernise you were with young John there.' I introduced Garnett as my 'Uncle Edward' and a look of disbelief spread over the man's face. Locally we were looked upon as 'furriners' and I had been asked several times whether it was true that my father was a 'seaman' which I corrected by saying he was a 'captain'. The man said:

'Ho – but you doan' look like no furriner to me if you forgive me sayin' so.'

Garnett explained that he was an 'adopted Uncle' as he was a friend of Mr Conrad who lived at Capel House.

'Oh – Ah – proper kind gen'l'mun, give me couple of bob t'other day, listened to me real friendly like, 'e did.' Garnett and I exchanged glances, a two-bob bit changed hands and we went on our way. Uncle Edward was curious about the man calling me 'Young John' and wanted to know if any of the other men around the farm spoke of, or to me, in the same way. I had not given it a thought but said I thought they did though why I had no idea perhaps they had heard JC call me 'Young scamp'. The fact remains that the epithet has stayed with me ever since, all through my professional life as an architect and even now that I am retired, old bricklayers, carpenters, plumbers and other craftsmen address me as 'Young John'.

Walking with Garnett or rather leading him through the woods was a rather sedate occupation, no scrambling up and down steep banks or crawling through hedges or undergrowth. He did not enjoy that sort of exertion so after the excitement of setting out I would settle down to a steady pace calling his attention to anything of interest. He was not a keen naturalist but he always showed an interest and his observations were stimulating so I was encouraged to ask questions or make remarks.

Not far away, about two and a half miles, at Leacon Hall, Warehorne, lived Sir John and Lady Millais, his mother, who became frequent visitors. Sir John was in the Navy and when he came home on leave he made a point of coming over to talk with my father who enjoyed his company. Sometimes he would bring his mother to see mine. On summer evenings he would come over and take us for a drive in his car, a Crossley, which ran very smoothly and with his sympathetic driving our progress was peaceful and relaxing. In those days it was something of an event if one met another car or a horse and trap.

One afternoon Millais arrived to ask JC if I could be spared to help him build a bridge across the middle of a pond that formed the south boundary of the kitchen garden at Leacon Hall. My father was delighted at the idea and after telling me to be useful and obedient he watched us depart down the drive. It never occurred to me as we left that I should be returning in a very short time soaking wet from head to foot having fallen into the pond within minutes of our arrival. JC treated it as a joke saying that the one thing he had forgotten to tell me was not to fall in. However, later on I was allowed to put the finishing touches to the bridge and in due course JC came to inspect it, questioning Millais closely as to whether I had been a help and if what I had done was satisfactory. Poor Millais – he was often laid up for a week or more with tuberculosis and eventually he was invalided out of the Royal Navy.

He had had the roof of the oast-house, situated to the southwest of the main house, repaired, and the cowl removed from the kiln which gave it a rather 'bald' appearance and it was this that prompted my father to suggest that a weathervane would look well on top of the conical roof. A short while later Millais came to see my father with a roll of paper under his arm and explained that he had decided to have a weathervane made in the form of a sailing ship and would appreciate JC's help with the design so that it was correct. The drawing was unrolled on the dining-room table and I can remember how important I felt standing by the table in that rather dim room while they discussed ideas and, whether it should be a 'full rigged ship' or a 'barque', finally deciding on a ship. It was after this that I came to appreciate JC's little 'match-stick and ink' sketches to a greater extent. How I regret not having kept them instead of letting my father screw them into a ball and drop them into the waste-paper basket.

Millais was a sick man when we first met him, his health steadily deteriorated and he died while still quite young. My father was very upset at his passing, missing his friendship and the tales of experiences in the Navy.

Arthur Symons, who lived at Wittersham, often came over to see us and we paid him the occasional visit, but I have the impression that my father rather tended to keep him at 'arms length' and he never became a close friend. He seemed to me to be a lonely person who lacked the ability to become a companion. Maybe I misjudge him, perhaps I was too young to appreciate his conversation, quite apart from the fact that our interests were totally different.

A minor fracas occurred that has remained in my memory partly because I was the centre of the disagreement between Symons and my father and partly because it amused me to hear my father ticking off someone. I had been showing Symons my 'ships' and expressed a wish that they were 'real' without explaining that I meant professionally made toys. He upbraided me for always dreaming of the impossible, for not being satisfied with what I had and for not realising that I wasted my father's time by asking to be amused or to be told things about ships and places which 'you promptly forget'. JC must have heard most of what was said and explained with heavy sarcasm that I was his son and if he chose to waste his time informing me of this or that it was his, JC's, business and no one else's. It was not until I was in my teens that I appreciated JC's way of ticking off a person. At Capel I could tell by the tone of voice without really understanding the words that he was displeased but I noticed in later

Mrs Conrad, Joseph Conrad and John in the drawing room at Capel House

years how people did not immediately realise just how scathing he could be.

Symons, like a number of my father's friends of those days gave me the impression of being envious of JC's ability without really appreciating the amount of mental effort and energy that my father put into his work. He was a hard taskmaster to himself: his work had to satisfy the high standard that he had set himself and he had to justify his existence and be worthy of the regard and esteem of his closest friends.

It was about this time that Will Cadby came to take photographs of my father who disliked being posed – it was a very real ordeal for him, particularly if he was being photographed by a stranger.

Joseph Conrad and John in driveway at Capel House

Moreover the process was a closed book to him technically. Lunch had been finished for some time and I was wondering what I was going to do that afternoon when I heard my father call, 'Hey, you there, Scamp, come here will you?' I ran into the drawing room where he was talking to Mr Cadby and immediately became aware of suppressed annoyance as he turned to me and said:

'I want you to give me your moral support. I must have your moral support this afternoon otherwise I shall not stand this damned business.' As they finished drinking their coffee Cadby explained that he wanted us to walk round the garden and when he called on us to 'stand' we were to stay motionless until he told us to move again. Unfortunately he did not realize that neither of us knew anything about exposures or light or in fact anything to do with cameras. He was lucky with the first photo, of my mother holding a coffee cup while I sat on the arm of JC's chair, because the sun came from behind a cloud and the light was strong enough for only a short exposure to be necessary. JC didn't like the idea of 'strutting round the house to be shouted at at odd moments.' We paraded round the drive and along the moat pausing every now and again when called upon to do so and, after about an hour and a half, turned back to the house much to JC's relief.

The photo of the three of us in the drawing room is the best of the indoor ones, though the ones taken in the dining room are good considering the difficulties presented by the poor natural light in that room rendered even worse by the clouds scudding across the sun. The only outdoor photograph that was any good was that of my father and myself with airgun, standing on the drive with the house in the background taken towards the end of our perambulation on our way indoors. My father was getting decidedly touchy by now at being shouted at and I could not resist the temptation to look at him to see if there was going to be an 'explosion'. We had been halted a number of times before this and both men's tempers were getting frayed since either JC and I did not stop immediately we were called to a halt or we had moved while the exposure was being made, or a cloud passed across the sun; it was a difficult and not very harmonious business.

The annoyance shows mostly in the photos taken indoors, the card game had to be 'held' for quite a long time while a cloud hid the sun and cast a shadow making the length of the exposure very hard to judge. The photo of my parents sitting either side of the fireplace in the dining room, with me leaning against my mother, is the most 'posed' and least natural as we never sat round this fireplace because it smoked! JC sitting alone by the fire was a lucky 'spur of the moment' snap as a break in the clouds allowed Cadby to use a short exposure. As far as I can recall these were the only photographs taken at Capel House 'by appointment'. Although several photographers asked to be allowed to come, I do not believe they ever did. Previously to Cadby's visit photos had been taken by Alfred Knopf and James Huneker but neither of them had come specifically to take photographs. Cadby's camera was an early type of plate camera with cap over the lens in place of a shutter and had to be set upon a wooden tripod, all of which helped to make it more tedious.

Vaguely across the backcloth of memory the shadow, it is nothing more, of Norman Douglas passes. About him I remember little save that he was always friendly and kind to me. His son, Robert, spent many school holidays with us at Capel and later when we lived at Spring Grove at Wye, near Ashford. I enjoyed their visits because Norman was an interesting person, who had travelled about on the continent and had many amusing anecdotes to relate. He spent a lot of time with his son and me in the garden and fields around Capel. At first I was called into the house so as to leave father and son together but Norman soon realised what was happening and I was called to join them. He was a large man with a quiet voice and never seemed to move very quickly. He was very thoughtful and considerate and tried to make as little work as possible for my mother when he came to stay. In his endeavours to save my mother trouble on one visit he got up after a bout of 'flu before he had recovered sufficiently, and we had to call in the gardener and another man to carry him upstairs again to the sick bay. I began to notice that certain of my father's friends caused my mother to become mildly jealous if they did not spend some time talking with her; most of them brought her a gift or a bunch of flowers or a copy of their latest book but she felt a little 'left out' if she did not have a tête-à-tête with each one.

Mr Roland Oliver, as he then was, often came over to have a talk with my father from his cottage which he had built about half a mile away. If JC was busy Mr Oliver would offer to take me for a walk through the woods. I enjoyed these rambles and learnt a lot from him, particularly about walking over other peoples' properties, shutting gates and not damaging fences or hedges. We would watch the

Joseph Conrad by fireplace in dining room at Capel House

Ford Maddox Heuffer (Ford), 1909

wild life and the estate workmen setting a new gatepost or lopping a tree, and once or twice we would visit the keeper at his hut in the woods and be shown the various traps he used and be given a handful of corn to throw into the pheasant pen. It was under the watchful eye of Mr Oliver that I was given my first instruction on how to layer a hedge by pulling out the rubbish with a 'hooking' tool, but I did not finish the course chiefly because I was too small and hadn't the strength to weave the 'plashers' down between the uprights.

I must confess that being taken through the woodland by the owner, whilst enjoyable, was devoid of any excitement and I much preferred going on my own or with a schoolboy friend. I am sure Mr Oliver knew that I wandered over his land which was, no doubt, why he took such pains to instruct me in the care of the countryside and I have always been grateful for that.

. . . . .

Ford Maddox Hueffer took very little notice of me when we lived at Aldington, I was only three and he made no attempt to ingratiate himself. It was not until after we had moved that I really became aware of him through his thoughtless and selfish attitude towards my mother which aroused my enmity. He was apparently unable to realise that not only was she lame but also in continuous discomfort from her knee.

During one of his first visits to Capel House he asked me to get something for him and when I gave it to him he did not thank me. I remember Violet Hunt snapping at him for not doing so, only to be glared at with a muttered reply that I ought to be thankful that I didn't get a box on the ears for being so long. She tried to console me by promising to send me a copy of her book 'Cats', which she did, inscribed to 'John Alexander Conrad from Violet Hunt Hueffer, Xmas, 1911–12'. I often heard scraps of gossip when my mother and her sister spoke about Hueffer's affaires with various women but I was too young to appreciate their comments. I could not understand how my mother put up with his lack of manners particularly when it seemed that I was always being told what were good and what were bad manners.

I remember after breakfast one day when he seemed to be singularly ill-mannered and complained that there had not been enough food for him, ignoring the fact that he had arrived, uninvited, just before supper the previous evening. He shouted at me 'Fetch my slippers.' I looked at him. 'Go on, fetch my slippers.' I moved nearer to the door, put my tongue out at him and said, 'Say please', and bolted for the relative safety of the garden. An hour or so later I wanted something from the house and without thinking twice went in to fetch it from the dining room. He pounced on me from behind the door and gave me a thrashing over his knee from which he only desisted when JC, appeared and told him just what he thought of him. From that time onwards JC's attitude to him changed and his visits became less frequent and when he did come he let us know in good time so that there was sufficient food for him. I never understood why JC put up with his boorish behaviour unless it was that my father felt beholden to him for letting us have the cottage at Aldington. He was never welcomed as JC's other friends were and there was an atmosphere of unease when he invited himself. I can remember my father asking my mother if she had any idea why he had come.

I confess that I took any opportunity to bedevil his existence when he was staying with us and one evening at dinner an occasion arose which was too good to miss. We had had the first course and my mother had collected the plates to take to the kitchen and I had made a great to-do of opening the door for her after staring at Hueffer who was sitting close to it. As I returned to my chair he got up. I glanced at JC and sat down, fully expecting a box on the ears – I had made it very plain to him that I thought he should have opened the door for my mother. But no, he solemnly stretched over the table, broke the wax runners off the candles and ate them. I could feel JC's foot pressing on mine but this was too much altogether – I looked him straight in the face and said, 'There is some more food to come Mr Hueffer.'

My father never said a word and I dared not look at him. The silence was only broken when my mother sat down again after bringing in the next course. Towards the end of his visits he took to ignoring me completely but it did not worry me and I never 'danced attendance' when he arrived, although JC always expected me to be with him when guests arrived. Hueffer was the exception to the injunction delivered at breakfast time when they were expected 'I want you to be present when they come aboard.'

Hueffer never became a close friend and I recall hearing my father say to my mother, after one of the last visits he made, 'He wants another tow – another book in collaboration – those days are over as far as I am concerned.'

There were times when I was 'shooed' out of the room while my mother tried to be a 'Solomon' and decide who was right, JC or Hueffer, when they had disagreed about a word or a phrase. Each put his side of the case to my mother and left her to decide. Needless to say my father was rarely wrong but there were the odd occasions when it was politic to decide otherwise. I honestly believe she tried to be impartial but there had to be periods of disagreement and whenever I read *The Inheritors* or *Romance* I am aware of a sense of irritation behind the written words like the presage of a storm.

JC was a sympathetic listener and looking back I have a strong impression that some of his acquaintances abused that friendliness and sympathy and in one or two instances definitely took advantage of his generosity. I think Hueffer found talking to my father helped to restore his confidence, and his rudeness and lack of manners might well have been due to a form of inferiority complex that developed

when he was alone or lacked anyone of comparable intelligence with
whom to converse.

On reflection there seem to have been three friends whose attention
to me upset my father in a mild way, a sort of mild jealousy which I
do not think he would have found easy to put into words. Garnett,
Cunninghame Graham and Curle nearly always came to stay by
themselves, one at a time, JC preferred to have them singly so that he
could give his undivided attention to each. Cunninghame Graham,
'Don Roberto' as my parents called him, and Richard Curle usually
arrived in time for lunch and expected me to take them for a walk in
the afternoon. Garnett more often came by the afternoon train and
would want his walk the following morning. I did not realise JC's
anxiety while we were away and it was not until I had been told how
he used to walk up and down in front of the house that I became
aware of it. When he saw us coming he would go indoors and then
come out to meet us on the doorstep. Inevitably we were always a
little longer than he expected and he would reproach me for keeping
our guest out too long. They came to my rescue and took the blame
which was accepted, albeit rather grudgingly. Later, when we were
alone, my father would remind me that he did not like his guests kept
out so long. They tried to get him to come with us but he always had
'a few things to attend to' and he never came. As far as I know he
never walked outside the boundaries of the garden at Capel except
on very rare occasions when he came to look at my boats on the
round pond in the field about eighty yards from the north end of the
moat.

One day Cunninghame Graham and I had been for a walk and
had been quite a bit further than usual and were met by a very
annoyed JC who ticked me off pretty sharply. I apologised but my
father was not at all pacified and after a few remarks about being
thoughtless told me to make myself scarce. Don Roberto tried to
make amends but JC said he was surprised at a grown man being led
astray by a small boy, a rather incongruous remark in the heat of the
moment which Don Roberto let pass with the suspicion of a wink at
me. I wandered off feeling somewhat disgruntled and assured myself
that I would not take another guest for a walk as I began to climb the
'foremast' pine at the end of the drive. About half way up the trunk a
group of branches grew out almost horizontally forming a sort of long
seat to which I often retired to rest or daydream. It was a hot

afternoon and we had walked quite a long way so after a bit I dozed off as I had done several times before.

Vaguely I became aware of a pressure on my shoulder and a voice saying, 'Come on, Jackilo, time for tea. Come down carefully.' I opened my eyes and saw Don Roberto looking down at me and seeing my surprise he said, 'You are not the only one to climb trees.'

I followed him to the ground and we went into tea and when we had finished my father called me to his room, lifted me onto his knee and said, 'You must know that I get anxious when you are out so long and so does your mother. There are too many damned holes full of water around here and you could easily get into difficulties. You must realise that our friends feel a responsibility for your safety so it behoves you to act sensibly and not take chances.' After that I had to tell JC where we were going but this was bound to be rather vague and I doubt if it would have been much real use.

Over the years Cunninghame Graham became a close friend but for some reason he was never given the title of 'uncle'. My parents always addressed him as Don Roberto. To me however he was always Mr Cunninghame Graham. He was a striking person with penetrating eyes and a certain haughtiness of manner which belied his friendliness and warmth. Always perfectly turned out, whether riding in the Row, or walking in the country or London, his attire was immaculate. A great and experienced horseman, he was a bit disappointed in me as I did not take any interest in horses and after one or two attempts to create an interest he accepted that fact. Both my father and I were 'put on a horse' while very young and, speaking for myself, I was jolly glad when I was lifted off. It is possible that this experience may have prejudiced me.

Every Christmas Cunninghame Graham sent me a book, either about engineering or exploration, signed with his almost illegible signature which looked to me as though he had had only just enough time to sign his name before the book was snatched away for posting. Whenever we went to London we were invited to tea at Mrs Dummett's, a very close friend of Don Roberto's, where we met our other friends who lived in London.

Arthur Marwood was a particular friend of my father and they spent many hours together, which puzzled me when I began to take notice of their frequent meetings. If Marwood had been in the Merchant Navy it would have seemed to me to be a natural friendship but he

R. B. Cunninghame Graham

was a farmer and as such it seemed odd because JC took no interest in farming or agriculture. It was several months after we moved to Capel that I realised that being a farmer did not imply a one track existence and that farmers frequently had other interests in life. I realise now that Marwood, besides being a sound critic, was also an excellent 'sounding board' for my father as he was not a member of the literary world and had no ambitions as an author. My father and Marwood visited each other on alternate weeks and when it was our turn to visit Water Farm at Stowting we harnessed our pony, Jenny, to the trap and drove the ten miles or so to the long low farmhouse by the stream at the foot of the Downs. Most times we went through Clap Hill and Brabourne and returned through Aldington where we called at Slingby's farm for eggs and butter. We nearly always stayed for 'tea', a Gargantuan meal set out on a long table in, as I recall, a rather dark and gloomy kitchen lit by a pair of oil lamps suspended from the ceiling. There was always far more food than we could eat, even allowing for the fact that we did not sit down to it until six o'clock; it was a real high tea taking the place of the tea and supper which we usually had at home.

After our move to Capel, Marwood used to cycle over to see us every fortnight but he was a victim of tuberculosis and as his strength began to fail he drove over in a dogcart drawn by a light but sturdy horse from the farm. He would arrive just before lunch to be met by my father and ushered straight into the drawing room. Come to think of it he was the only other person for whom my father did not expect me to be 'in attendance when he arrived'. Now that was another facet of my father's behaviour; as I have stated he expected me to be with him to welcome friends but certain of them, Hueffer, Marwood and Garnett, had to be met when they 'arrived' whereas others like Graham, Hope, Curle, Gibbon and Douglas were met when they 'came aboard'. I was never aware of my father making notes of these peoples arrivals so one is justified in assuming that it was another example of his amazingly retentive mind.

When Marwood came to see us my father wore his every-day 'rig' of grey flannels, waistcoat and jacket but when he went to Stowting he was more particular and wore a Norfolk jacket and trousers usually of tweed and leather 'leggings' which fitted over the tops of his boots, which were either black or brown but in any case brilliantly polished. My mother spent her time talking to Mrs, or was it Miss, Marwood? I never found out though I rather fancy she was his

Arthur Marwood

sister. I was sent out to amuse myself round the farm with a host of instructions not to do this, that or the other. Apart from being told not to get wet, there was no injunction to keep away from the stream which ran along the fence in front of the house and so I spent most of my time there. It was nearly always late in the evening before we left to go home and I can remember watching the harness gleaming in the light of the side lamp and then opening my eyes to the light coming from the front door at Capel, having slept for most of the journey. I remember one night when we stayed until almost midnight when Mr Marwood had been telling us about a certain house nearby, past which a horse could not be driven at midnight on midsummer night. My father was rather amused at the seriousness with which Marwood told the tale and decided to stay on and go round past the house on our way home as it would only be about a mile further. We harnessed the pony and set off along the lane at the foot of Cobb Hill, timing our departure so as to arrive at the drive entrance to the house at midnight. We approached the gate in bright moonlight and the pony became more and more nervous and finally stopped about twenty-five or thirty yards short of the gate across the entrance. After several attempts to drive past JC got down and tried to lead the animal past but it reared up and nearly deposited my mother and me in the roadway. My father tried persuasion but Jenny was not going to pass that entrance for anyone and at last JC gave way to my mother's entreaties and turned round to drive home by our usual route. Whether it was because the pony had had a good feed and a long rest or whether it decided that that was not our normal way home or whether there was some apparition which the pony saw or sensed we never did find out. Personally I think that the animal did see or feel something that frightened her as she broke out in a sweat but she never refused at any other time and she had been past that entrance many times in daylight.

The story was that many years ago the then owner of the property returned unexpectedly to find his wife with a gentleman friend in compromising circumstances. A fight with swords ensued during which the gentleman friend was beheaded by the husband, who placed the body on the friend's horse, put the head under the corpse's arm and sent it off into the night. And so it appears each midsummer night.

Arthur Marwood was very lenient with me if I got into mischief but he never went out of his way to be more than just friendly. He was a big man with a happy disposition and a pleasant voice, but rather slow and methodical in his movements. My father looked forward to their weekly meetings for although he never became an intimate friend, knowing all the family affairs, he was a very close friend with whom my father could discuss his work. The fact that he was not a 'literary animal' made his comment and opinions far more useful than they would otherwise have been for he was able to give a reader's point of view. My father took only a 'friendly' interest in the

day-to-day happenings at Marwood's farm, going to see a newly-
born calf or a litter of pigs but he never showed any real enthusiasm
for any branch of farming.

Jack and Ada Galsworthy came to see us often and were always very
gladly received by my parents who enjoyed their company. However
there seemed to be a barrier between me and them, which worried
me for a time since I could not think of anything that I had done to
cause a rift. I accept that they came to see my parents but their
attitude to me was so different from JC's other friends, that I had the
impression that Galsworthy was on the look out all the time in case I
should perpetrate some mischief. I knew better than to make a scene
if I thought people were ignoring me and more often than not I was
glad to be left to my own devices and not be fussed over. I looked
upon their visits with mixed feelings and was always on my best
behaviour in deference to JC's obvious enjoyment of their company.
I felt constrained to behave well but I was never conscious of this
feeling with my father's other friends.

The feeling of being watched the whole time I was in the room with
them was not conducive to friendship; it was too much like the 'ogre'
in the cottage at Aldington. It was once suggested that this attitude
might have been engendered because I was born in their house
which they lent my parents for the event and Galsworthy was upset
by my father's description of me as 'quiet, unassuming and
extremely ugly'. The fact does remain that we were never more than
acquaintances though he, partly, fulfilled his duty as a godfather by
sending me a book each Christmas, until I went to school, inscribed
'To Master John Conrad from Mr Galsworthy'. With this wide
chasm between us I think I did my duty by writing to thank him and
that was where our acquaintance ended. I never did discover any
reason for the distance between us and after my father's death, when
I was driving my mother about visiting old friends, their house
seemed barred to me. After leaving my mother with them I would be
told to come back in two or three hours and if she had been invited to
lunch it did not include me. At the time it did not seem so very
unnatural but, looking back, one cannot help wondering why it was.
I have a clear conscience though it is possible that I might have asked
to be excused. In any event I do not remember doing so.

Ernest and A. J. Dawson often came over from Rye to see us but we never knew how they would come. Sometimes they would travel by rail to Hamstreet and walk across the fields from the corner of the lane to the Church, or by motorbike and sidecar and once in a Raleigh Tricar. This consisted of a wickerwork armchair mounted between the two front wheels of the tricycle with the afterpart of a motor-cycle attached to it. It was a means of conveyance, just, but totally unsuitable for Ernest, who was tall, large and broad and who completely filled the 'armchair' while his brother, short, lean and wiry peeped over his shoulders from his seat on the saddle behind. I remember JC throwing up his hands in amazement when they came to a halt in front of the house. They soon parted with it as its shortcomings became apparent for two persons so dissimilar in size. They were very real friends of the family and while one would talk to my father, the other talked to my mother or got me to take him round the garden. And if it was AJ who was with me I had a job on my hands trying to keep Hadji, our dog, from knocking him over – he was very fond of dogs and had written a book about them but Hadji's exuberance was quite extraordinary. Prior to their arrival there was no sign of the animal but before they had had time to shake hands he hurled himself at AJ, evading all at stopping him. Ernest had been in the judiciary in India and AJ was in the Army and between them they had much to tell my father about their experiences in the East. The fascination for that part of the world stayed with JC to the end of his life.

It was in 1912 that Richard Curle first came to see my father and the friendship that developed between them was unique and unequalled by any other friendship. It was built on trust, the best possible foundation. It was complete; there were no secrets and there was a total confidence between them. My father found in Dick Curle the mental stimulus that he expected from his closest friends. He was a sympathetic and understanding friend and was able to attune his mind to whatever subject was under discussion with the exception of anything mechanical about which he knew nothing and cared little. He was a frequent and much appreciated visitor to our house right up to the time of his death. I have seen and heard him hold an audience without any apparent effort using the same words as in his books and yet I do not find his books interesting though I have been entranced listening to him. Curle could tell a story, describe a place or create an atmosphere and had travelled extensively with 'both eyes open' as JC often remarked.

It was not long before he became Uncle Dick to me and we were close friends for the rest of his life. There were periods of huff when I had said something that sounded critical which he took exception to, and occasionally I misinterpreted the advice given in one of his many letters, but I am glad to say that these spells did not last long. I believe in every case they were due to misunderstandings and if he did get cross with me I probably deserved it – I do not deny that I can be cussed at times.

When I was small he used to perform various tricks for my amusement such as making a coin disappear or balancing a walking stick on the toe of his shoe and if my father thought that I was going to forget to say 'thank you' he would clap his hands or make some remark to remind me. Dick liked Capel House because it was a quiet place in a world that had not then become noisy. It was far enough from the road to be undisturbed by the small amount of traffic that passed along the lane. It was primitive by today's standards – no electricity, no telephone, no hot water and only cold from a massive tap in the kitchen – but it was a friendly place which my father was sorry to leave. My mother's placid disposition helped to create a relaxed atmosphere which never seemed boring to our friends. Dick Curle appreciated both that and my mother's cooking – she enjoyed preparing a meal to which justice would be done but it had to be something very special before JC enthused about it.

8

Mother cooking – typing – food – preferences –
Nellie Lyons – foreign visitors – illness – no slacking
– Dr Tebb – Dr Mackintosh – Dr Fox – dentist –
comedy – mannerisms – eyeglass – accent – Lear –
Carroll – verse

When you have grown up with someone who is lame there is a
tendency to take his or her misfortune for granted and it was not until
I was about eight or so that I became aware of my mother's fortitude
and the way she always managed to keep cheerful in spite of the pain
in her damaged knee. There is no doubt in my mind that she suffered
from almost continuous wearying pain but she would stand over the
cooker for as long as necessary to prepare a meal, leaning against the
jamb of the opening, holding a candlestick in one hand while she
stirred a saucepan with the other.

There were times when she had been typing all day to get an
article or story off to the publishers, when JC's visits to the den to see
how she was progressing proved too much and her stoicism gave way
in a flood of tears. Poor dear – she could not storm out of the house
and it was not her nature to fly off the handle. She could not ask
Nellie Lyons to prepare a meal as the latter's knowledge of cooking
was very limited and JC would not have eaten it, so my mother tried
to 'get back on an even keel' by preparing some rather special dish for
my father. I think he knew when life got a 'bit too near the wind' and
my mother had been 'blown off course' but there was never any show
of marital affection in front of me apart from a tender pat on her
shoulder and a muttered endearment.

My father could be quite difficult over meals not to his liking, and
he could be a little unreasonable over badly cooked food demanding
that it be 'properly cooked next time' when it was sent back to the
kitchen. He had a strong preference for French cooking, more
especially for the traditional dishes of the Mediterranean coast. He
was very fond of hot dishes, hot curry that made one perspire over the
eyelids, horseradish sauce made rather sweet, tabasco and pimen-

toes, and any other hot substances; and heaven help anyone who served soggy rice. He had a weakness for ravioli, risotto, gnocchi, and mushroom omelettes but he would only eat mushrooms that had been gathered round the house. If any risotto was left after an evening meal he always gave instructions that it was to be kept and warmed up for his breakfast. He loathed porridge for which he had a variety of names: 'damned fish glue', 'blasted frog spawn', 'Revolting! Like uncooked dough'. His antipathy to it was largely due to the uninviting colour and consistency of the usual hotel variety of those days. Certain of our friends were known to like it for breakfast, Dick Curle for one, to whom it was always served to a special recipe of his own. Though my mother made bread sauce in a special way which was acceptable, JC never really liked it any more than he liked a boiled chicken, which he considered to be a waste of good food.

I did not take much interest in the running of the house though I was occasionally called by my mother to fetch something from the larder usually as a last resort when our maid, Nellie Lyons, was absent or could not find what she had been asked to get. She was a kind person and always willing, but my parents did find her annoying at times and let her know it. Nevertheless she took it in good spirit and tried even harder to please and was always nearby if anyone needed comforting. I have grateful memories of her as she would go out of her way to warn me if someone was after me for leaving my clothes lying about or not putting my shoes away. It would be 'Hi, master Jack you come and put your shoes away and hang up your coat' – frequently just in time for me to do the necessary job before being called into the drawing room to be ticked off.

We had our misfortunes with domestic helps and maids, chiefly because they were not warned that some of our visitors might come from abroad. I remember a new maid had just started work in the house when a Polish friend came to see my father. When he rang the bell she answered the door. Instead of asking for Mr Conrad he said, 'Pan Korzeniowski is here, yes?'. To which the girl replied 'No sir, no one of that name here, sir', and shut the door. It was not until he got back to Ashford station that he realised his mistake and came back again to see my father. After this my father insisted that if the person answering the door could not understand what was said they were to ask the visitor to write their name and message, if any, on a paper pad which was to be kept by the front door.

This worked quite well until a temporary maid was helping us out when one of our regular staff was away. In addition to being rather nervous she was also a little slow witted. She had been told about getting people to write their name on the pad if she didn't understand what they said so, when the door-bell rang, she went to answer it. A long low-pitched conversation was heard taking place, and then she was heard knocking on the door of my father's room. More conversation and then JC stormed out, 'What is this? Damn fool girl brings me a piece of paper with a cross on it and says she doesn't know what the man wants.' JC went to the door where he was confronted by an unwashed and rather unsavoury tramp asking for alms. My father gave him some money and sent him on his way and then told the girl to use her head another time and not bother him with tramps.

It seemed to me that unless my father was totally incapacitated by gout he was a trying patient and used his own interpretation of the doctor's instructions, frequently stopping the treatment as soon as there was the slightest improvement in his condition as he seemed to begrudge every moment he was ill and unable to work. It often happened that he tried to get back to work before he had regained his strength and well-being with the result that he had a relapse so that an illness that might have come and gone in days lingered on for weeks. He hardly ever took anything to make him sleep though he did take caffeine or phenacetin sometimes to relieve gouty pains but only very sparingly. If he had a chill he would take ten to fifteen drops of chlorodyne though he was never one to take medicine unless very definitely needed.

When he was at sea there was always plenty of physical activity to keep him occupied and he was less aware of aches and pains. There is no doubt in my mind that the sea air was very beneficial to him. When he took up writing he lost the physical exertion and the sea air that would have done him good after his Congo adventure (see the 'Congo Diary' in *Tales of Hearsay and Last Essays*). He did not seem to be able to relax and even when he appeared to be resting in a chair there was great mental activity going on the whole time. He never called attention to his own industry, though the fact remains that anyone who came in contact with him in every-day life responded to his example and none of the crew dawdled during working hours. If a farmhand came to the door to ask a question he would say as soon as he had the answer, 'Well I'll be getting on, the Guv'ner won't want to see me hanging about.' Yet he was not a slave driver.

Dr Tebb was one of the first English doctors whom my father consulted but I only became aware of him after we moved to Capel House when their friendship had become established, although I believe he brought me into the world. It took several visits for a new doctor to be accepted by my father and my mother would advise whoever came not to start 'doctoring' straight away but rather to get round to it gradually. Dr Tebb's youngest son, Cuthbert, often spent part of his school holidays with us and I was glad of his company because there were no other boys of my own age living nearby.

Another doctor of those days was Dr Mackintosh who came to see my mother and try various treatments for her damaged knee. He remained a close friend for many years and at one time in the First World War I lived with him for a while and was given a job in the foundry in which he had an interest, carrying the sand moulds from one part to the other for pouring.

After we moved to Capel Dr Fox became our medical adviser, and continued to look after my father for the rest of his life. In those days a doctor became a close friend of the family and when there was an illness there was an etiquette to be followed. On arrival he was taken straight up to the patient, in whose room a wash basin with a can of hot water, soap and a towel were provided. When he had made his diagnosis and had had a wash he was taken down to the drawing room where whisky and soda or a bottle of wine and biscuits had been set out, and my father or mother would sit and talk while he took some refreshment. If he called at meal time he was always asked to join us at table. Dr Fox tried very hard to get my father to have his teeth attended to and often carried his persuasion to the point of almost having a row but my father was very stubborn and would not take his advice.

This recalls an occasion when my father had toothache, and an appointment had been made with a dentist in Ashford whose house was on the north side of Bank Street. As he always had to have a companion with him on these visits my father took me with him and, as was his habit, he insisted on leaving much sooner than necessary, even allowing for the unreliability of the car. So we had a long time to wait. JC decided that we would walk up and down until it was time to go in so we walked down to the corner of Church Road, turned and walked back past the dentist's house to Burrow's estate agency and then back again. I saw from the clock over the office door that the time for the appointment had passed and called my father's attention to it, 'Oh, that's all right, the fellow before us has not come out yet.'

Another period of walking up and down and then my father said, 'We will go home now. It has stopped aching.' Although he never referred to any experience of primitive dentistry as practised aboard ship, I can't help thinking that something of this kind might have been an explanation for his dread of the dentist's chair. We all know that sinking feeling when we sit back and open wide, and it does not matter how many people tell us how good a dentist he is, we are all disquieted. This particular dentist was known to be one of the most painless practitioners and did much for me when I had to go to him. When I was shedding my first teeth, JC would never stay in the room while a loose tooth was 'persuaded' to come out and was quite annoyed with my mother for sending me into his room to show him the tooth – there was no need to make a fuss about an ordinary natural process!

I learnt to keep a straight face as a small boy in spite of an almost overwhelming desire to laugh on some occasions. Once JC had taken a mouthful of cold water to ease an aching tooth when he forgot and opened his mouth to 'shoo' a cat away; he saw the funny side to it after he had changed his damp clothes. Another time he was going for a walk round the garden with a friend and we heard a great to-do while the friend waited outside. 'Where is the damned thing? I know I had it a moment ago.' I had to go and see what was happening and found my father on his knees poking about under the furniture with a walking stick. Seeing me he demanded that I should find his stick – I had a real job to keep a straight face while I pointed out that he had it in his hand which made him even more put out. Later on he had a good laugh at this kind of thing but at the time – *mille tonnere*!

I always knew when he was going to tell an amusing anecdote or story as he had a trick of hooking the first finger of his right hand over his nose as he approached the climax of the tale. If, on the other hand, he was listening to a funny story which was particularly amusing he would slap his right leg a resounding blow. He enjoyed stories that were really funny but had no time for anything that was indecent though he was not a prude and often bought *La vie parisienne* and, for light reading in English, *Punch*. He liked debate and interesting argument and as he became more immersed in the conversation he would cross his legs, right over left, and then tuck his right foot round behind his left calf. If the person he was talking to began to ramble or become boring his foot would slip from behind his calf and be agitated from side to side. When he was in deep thought during a pause in the conversation he would twiddle his thumbs at an amazing speed, first one way and then the other. In later years when we played chess his thumb-twiddling was an excellent guide for it became slower and slower as the moves became more subtle and excitement mounted. He would tap the side of his nose when he was about three moves off 'checkmate'.

Another trick that he used with considerable effect, especially if he found a visitor prying into his papers, was to blow his nose, not just an ordinary blow but a real trumpet and I remember seeing several inquisitive people really jump when they were caught in this way. Hueffer was one such person and he had the effrontery to complain when he was made to jump, and was told in no uncertain manner that he should mind his own business. This must have been to one of the last visits he made to us before we left for Poland, probably in the early part of the summer of 1914 because I remember seeing and hearing the interlude through the open window of the drawing room.

My father did get a bit short with some visitors, especially strangers, who said in conversation: 'As an author', or 'being an author do you think ...?' He would put up with the phrase for a while, then say, 'Yes, I am an author but I am also a human being. Pray don't forget that!' Some people thought that the eyeglass which he habitually carried was an affectation, but when quite young he had suffered an injury to his right eye from a whip and the eyeglass did help his vision. If a visitor was late arriving he would walk to and fro swinging the eyeglass like a pendulum or whirl it round and round according to the intensity of his anxiety. He was not conscious of this trick and broke a number of glasses against door jambs or pieces of furniture. He always bought three or four glasses at a time and each had to be threaded with a length of black cord and there were ructions if someone tied a 'granny' knot!

In retrospect I can't help wishing that I had been made to read aloud more frequently by someone who knew the art. My mother did not make any attempt to teach me and my aunt lacked any gift for teaching. JC would get me to read a few lines, then take the book to show me how to read, become engrossed and just go on reading, which he did well. I was not aware of his accent and I do not agree with statements made by some of his friends that he was difficult to understand; he would not have got his master's ticket or the respect of seamen if he had not been understandable. He had an accent but it was not nearly so obvious as some people made out, but like a number of Europeans he found the English 'th' troublesome and would say;- 'dis' and 'dat' for 'this' and 'that', or 'dose' for 'those' and he always referred to a 'sword' as a 'suword' making the 'w' very distinct.

He admired Edward Lear and would spend whole evenings reading the *Nonsense Songs and Stories*, and he was also very fond of the Lewis Carroll books. The verses in these seemed to have a particular attraction for him and he would read them through aloud several times. The 'Walrus and the Carpenter' was an early favourite as the local bricklayer was a perfect 'Walrus' and the local carpenter might have been the 'model' for Tenniel's dawing. 'You are old, Father William, the young man said' also had his counterpart in the village in the person of the butcher with snow white hair but the favourite was:

> They told me you had been to her,
> And mentioned, me to him – –

The poignancy of the memories of Capel, the drawing room with the yellow lamplight, the serenity, the peace and feeling of security – one treasures the memories and the experiences of those days though they are now so far away. If I go into a chandlers the picture of the ''tween decks' rises; with the smell of tarred rope, oil and pulley blocks that seemed to pervade the air in that room though, in fact, apart from the paraffin oil for the lamps and some odd lengths of rope there were no other maritime bits and pieces.

This smell of a ship's chandlers was remarked upon by Robert Douglas, younger son of Norman Douglas, who spent most of his school holidays with us when his father was abroad. I recall the day when Lord Northcliffe came to lunch and during the meal Robert had asked why there was a smell of the chandlers in the 'tween decks. This interested Northcliffe who asked if he might see the room after lunch, remarking that he had not had an opportunity to sample the 'smell of the ghost of a ship' before. JC was not amused but Northcliffe realised that he had been misunderstood and created a diversion by suggesting that Robert and I should be taken for a run in the Rolls Royce later on. There was ample room on the front seat for the driver and two excited schoolboys and soon we were being driven in smooth and stately silence along the roads of Romney Marsh.

I do not remember whether this was during a period when we were without a car or whether my mother persuaded Northcliffe to send his Rolls to fetch my parents for lunch at Margate where he was then living, but it turned up about a week later and they rolled away in a cloud of dust down the drive, returning in the late afternoon. They had thoroughly enjoyed their outing and my mother was most impressed by the smoothness of the ride – it was quite a trip in those days as very few people travelled nearly eighty miles between mid-day and six in the evening.

9

Poland – Hamburg – Berlin – Cracow – Gorski portrait – Vienna – Milan – Genoa – Gibraltar – Tilbury

25 July 1914 saw us leave, with Joseph Retinger and his wife, Tola, for a visit to Poland. The Retingers had been frequent visitors for the previous two years and it was an invitation from Tola Retinger's relations to stay with them on their estate just over the frontier in Russia, that persuaded my father to agree to the trip.

So we packed our cases and boarded the train for London where we had dinner before going on to Harwich to embark for Hamburg. I do not remember much of this trip though I do recall seeing the reflection of the lights round the harbour as we moved into the North Sea. The next day it was fairly rough and JC made me walk round the deck feeding me on apples which he maintained were a very effective way of reducing any tendencies to seasickness.

We were well into the Elbe before I went on deck the next morning to find my father and brother discussing the shipping passing up and down the river. I suppose there were signs of naval activities, perhaps of war, but I have no recollection of it. I think I must have been tired or not well as I remember very little of the journey and nothing at all, except that we went to the Hamburg Zoo, during the day. Later in the day or, perhaps the next morning, we went on to Berlin where we went for a drive round the city after depositing our luggage at an hotel. My father pointed out the various buildings and commented on the tidiness of the streets which he found unfriendly after those of English towns. It was while we were in Berlin that war was declared and I remember sitting through the lengthy discussions that preceded our departure for Cracow from where we hoped to be able to reach our destination.

I can recall the lights set high up in the blue haze of the station roof when we left Berlin in the late evening. The guard, whistle in hand, waited while my mother hurried along as best she could until we found a compartment where we could all be together. At last it was found and we stood waiting while my mother heaved herself up into the carriage, the floor of which was about level with my eyes. A lift and a shove by JC, and I was aboard, followed by my brother, the Retingers and my father. As the door slammed to, the train jerked into motion and so started one of the longest and most boring train journeys I have ever made. I must have slept for quite a long time in short snatches, waking occasionally and being vaguely conscious of passing through stations, hearing the regular beat of the rail joints, the rhythm suddenly shattered by a junction in the rails. Then there was a long stop around midnight, when it was blowing half a gale and raining in torrents, and most of the station lights were out or nearly so. Hundreds of soldiers seemed to be lined up beside the track; there was much shouting and clattering of arms, though it was only through the occasional flash of a torch or flare of a match that one realized how many men there were. I have no idea what town it was but I should think, most probably Breslau, as it is approximately midway between Berlin and Cracow.

Eventually we arrived at Cracow and managed to get room at an hotel. I have the impression that my mother and I were pretty well tired out by the journey and I was not well. I have only the haziest recollections of being shown round the town – the quadrangle of the university was filled with scaffolding and we had to clamber round blocks of stone and building materials to see the doorway through which my father passed on his way to his tutor many, many years before.

None of us felt any of the nostalgia that my father must have felt at that time, it was not 'the past' of our lives and not one of us, my mother, my brother nor I had an inkling of the poignancy of that moment for my father. I certainly did not appreciate or notice any show of feeling but then I was busy taking in what I saw.

The next day we went out to visit a friend of my father at his estate of Gorka Narodowa, in a carriage drawn by two horses. It was some distance from the town and I remember being impressed by the emptiness of the countryside and the feeling of loneliness that those rolling slopes without any dwellings created. Whilst we were at tea a servant came in and told our host that the army had arrived and was commandeering all the horses but luckily he managed to persuade them to leave our two so that we could get back to our hotel at Cracow.

We left Cracow on my eighth birthday, 2 August, and boarded the train for Zakopané. I do not know whether it was chance or my father's forethought but we had the last compartment of the last carriage of the train to ourselves. Looking out from the windows we were able to see the engine winding up the curves ahead and my father kept me fully occupied going from side to side to watch the engine negotiate the steep gradients. I remember being fascinated by the numerous rods and levers, the little whiffs of steam, and the beat of the exhaust as the engine toiled up the slope. My father told me that it was fitted with Walscheart's valve-gear, but that did not convey much to me at the time though in later years he explained its operation and that of other valve-gears; he knew quite a lot about steam engines and railways.

We arrived at Zakopané where the line terminated and after loading our belongings onto a horse and trap drove to Konstantynowka the house of Madame Zagorska, where we were to stay for the next two months. It was not our original intention to stay here but with the outbreak of war it was considered a fairly safe place to which to retire until the shape of things to come could be determined.

Konstantynowka was a 'pension' and typical of the other houses of this resort. It was built entirely of wood, clad with horizontal boards and lined with vertical matchboarding, full of knots and liberally varnished; enormous cast-iron and tiled stoves stood in each living room, throwing out a searing heat from the blazing logs with which they were filled. As the weather got colder the stoves were driven harder and the metalwork at the top and the smoke-pipe glowed red of an evening, when numerous friends came to talk in the crowded hall. The two lamps hanging from the ceiling beams only managed to produce an 'illuminated gloom' within the dark walls and under the layers of cigarette smoke floating above our heads. There must have been a guardian angel watching over us to protect us from fire. Why the house did not go up in flames will always be a mystery to me.

A continuous balcony or gallery ran round the house at each floor, about four feet wide, with stairways connecting them to one another on each side of the house – I spent hours rushing round and up and down. The ground floor and its balcony were about four feet above the earth and the other levels were about ten feet apart. The grounds of the house were separated from the footpath by a hedge and on the opposite side the pinewoods began at the edge of the road. Rushes and mosses grew by a tiny stream and here and there the gray mass of a lump of rock showed through.

While we were here my father agreed to let Doctor Gorski make a portrait of him. My father had very definite ideas about sitting for a portrait which were a little unusual, perhaps, in that he maintained that once he had taken up his pose he should not make any movement whatsoever. Because of this I was appointed cigarette boy. It was my duty to accompany him to the sitting, where I would sit near him with a packet of cigarettes and a box of matches. On a signal from him I would put a cigarette in his mouth and apply a light to it. I don't remember getting tired of this occupation, probably because I sat on the window seat and watched the doctor at work.

As the days went by Dr Gorski became a firm friend and took pity on a small boy, often calling in the afternoon and taking him for a walk in the pinewoods. He always came prepared with a large packet of peppermint creams and I think it was due to this apparently never ending supply of sweets that I became so fond of them.

Towards the end of the sittings my father decided that I should be rewarded for my patience and promised he would take me to the café on the other side of the square for a cup of chocolate. Perhaps I was not looking where I was going or, perhaps, the pavements were uneven but I fell over and cut my knee, making it bleed profusely. My father pulled out his silk handkerchief, which he always carried, and hastily bound up the wound saying that we would go to a chemist and have it properly bandaged. A short walk and we arrived at the shop. We took off our hats and my father passed the time of the day with the proprietor and then started into a long conversation. I listened patiently as I felt the blood trickle down my leg and into my shoe, soaking my sock. The conversation came to an end and my father turned to leave at which I said, 'What about my knee?' The effect was electrifying. Everyone started to rush around collecting bandages, hot water, ointments, disinfectants and anything else they could lay their hands on. Looking back I am amazed at the fuss that was made over what was a relatively minor wound and, although it bled profusely, it did not hurt much.

During our stay in Zakopané we made several trips along the roads into the mountains in an open trap drawn by a single horse. My mother enjoyed these trips as they helped to break the monotony of being house-bound by her injured knee. One afternoon we took a drive towards a mountain pass to see a famous waterfall which dropped a considerable height into a large hole at the side of the road from which there was no visible outlet, though it did not overflow. I was fascinated by this and asked my father numerous questions which he answered by explaining that the water passed into a subterranean stream and, after travelling a considerable distance underground, it joined the main river in the plains to the south of the mountains. Years later he set me the task of investigating a similar sort of mystery in the valley in which Oswalds stands.

From the window of my room at Konstantynowka I could see the top of Giewont, one of the peaks of the Tatry range of mountains on which a massive cross had been erected. I was curious to know how it got there and pestered my parents to let me go up the mountain with my brother and his friends when they decided to visit it one day. I was told it was too far for a small boy and so I had to be content with being told how the parts had been made in the village and then carried up to the top and put together there.

They were happy days at Konstantynowka in spite of minor illnesses and occasional earaches that afflicted me. I can see the 'salon' as the hall was called, filled with people, their faces indistinct through the tobacco smoke, the hot stuffy atmosphere created by the large wood-burning stove at the end of the room, and the endless chatter of friends who came each evening to talk with my father. I did not understand what it was all about but I enjoyed listening and watching the animation of some of the visitors who used their hands more than others to emphasise some point in the conversation.

I recall that same picture, though with many more people, on the evening of our departure: the ceiling of the salon no longer visible through the smoke, the pushing and apologising as people tried to move about the room. I was sitting by my mother on a divan near the stove trying to hear what a friend was saying in rather broken English when, suddenly, I was grabbed by the arm and towed through the crowd and out into the passage and up the stairs to the top of the house, to a little attic bedroom, where Cousin Angela told me to help her pull a large canvas trunk from under the bed. After much heaving and shoving we managed to get it out, and from a pile of papers she extracted one saying,

'I want to give you this. Take care of it. In years to come you will be glad I gave it to you. It is an etching of Cracow University quadrangle and shows the statue of Copernicus and behind it, to the right, is the door through which your father passed when he went to his tutor. It was drawn by a great friend of mine. In the left-hand corner he has made a little sketch of me at a writing table and in the right-hand corner a sketch of the house in which I lived.' We returned to the salon where my mother took the etching, rolled it round a piece of wood, and packed it in our trunk.

At last it was time to go and we left the lights and cigarette smoke and walked through a ravine of snow down to the road. Some four or five feet had fallen in the last few days but whoever cleared the snow away from our path had made a good job of it and my mother managed to negotiate the twenty yards or so to the carriage without mishap. We packed ourselves into the two-horse trap, our luggage piled up by the driver, and set off, soon after midnight, for the railway station from which we were to catch a train back to Cracow. We were given an immense sheepskin rug which smelt strongly of partly cured skins and was rather dirty, but the night was so cold that we tucked it round our legs and backs to help keep us warm. After about half an hour our suspicions about the rug were definitely confirmed and we started to itch but the scratching was, perhaps, a blessing in disguise as it helped to keep us from getting too cold – those fleas had a real feast. After what seemed to me a very long time we arrived at the railway station and boarded the train for the next stage of our journey to Vienna. I was told later that we spent a whole day waiting in the station at Cracow before being allowed to get on the train. When at last the train arrived it had many wounded soldiers on it but I must have fallen asleep as soon as we settled in the compartment since I remember nothing at all of that journey.

We arrived in the evening to find chaos everywhere but we did, eventually, get to our hotel where we found a message from some Polish friends who left Zakopané a few days before us.

After we had been shown our rooms and had had a wash my father took me aside and said, 'I want you to take a message to these friends who want to see us. When you have found their room, knock on the door and say to whomever opens it "Ojciec jest tutaj". Now don't forget, "Ojciec jest tutaj" – it means "father is here".'

Then resting his hand on my shoulder he took me out into the corridor, which was very high, very narrow and stretched away into the distance, lit by tiny electric light bulbs set close to the ceiling at

wide intervals. 'Now off you go and remember "Ojciec jest tutaj".'
After wandering round for some time, climbing stairs, traversing
corridors, I found the room and knocked on the door and delivered
my message. After a short while I led them back to our room where
my mother welcomed me like a long lost traveller, rather to my
father's annoyance. Apparently there had been a difference of
opinion about sending me off into the unknown regions of a foreign
hotel full of strangers but this aspect of the adventure did not occur to
me at the time; my father had told me to do something and that was
enough for me. In some strange way he seemed to impart a feeling of
confidence in people when he gave an order or made a request for
them to perform some service for him. One did not argue – one did as
one was told.

I believe we stayed about five days in Vienna while Mr Penfield,
the American Ambassador, made arrangements for the next stage of
our journey, but with the preparations for war going on around us,
we were unable to see any of the sights, in addition to which my
father was not well.

Vienna by this time was in a turmoil with the army everywhere
and when it was time for us to leave we were hustled out of the back
door of the hotel where we were confronted with a vast red touring
car, a Lorraine Diederichs, which was waiting to take us to the
station. The driver had insisted that the car should be brought to the
rear where there was less activity by the army as he feared it might be
commandeered if he came to the front of the hotel. The fear of having
his car taken was also given as the reason for the somewhat circuitous
route by which he took us to the station, in spite of being late leaving
and making it necessary to hurry. In later years when my father
spoke of that journey he described it by saying, 'The town spun
round us, the houses whirled and rushed away past us, only to be
followed by more.' It was quite the most hair-raising journey we ever
had – over pavements, round corners, the tyres letting out protesting
shrieks, pedestrians scattering in all directions in spite of the horn
being in constant use. We got to the station in one piece but whether
it was by good driving or good luck no one can say. What a car, what
a driver and what a journey!

As a result of that headlong rush we had ample time to board the
train for Milan and eventually mountains came in sight, but how
were we to get past that towering obstacle, relentlessly coming
nearer and nearer? Looking back I can smile at my anxiety, but at

the time it was quite a frightening experience intensified by the fact that no one else seemed to be the least worried. However my father soon realised that something was wrong and explained to me that we would soon be entering a tunnel and then went on to describe how it was built.

At the frontier station we disembarked to go through customs, and as soon as our luggage and passports had been cleared, my mother and I walked along the train that was to take us on to Italy. I looked round to see whether my father and brother were following and was surprised to see them making signs for us to hurry and get aboard as soon as possible. We got in and closed the door, and as the train moved off two German officers started to run after it shouting for the train to stop but they were too late; and so we escaped being interned until the end of the war.

We arrived in Milan and after we had found rooms in an hotel my father decided that it might relieve the tension if we took a drive round the town after dinner. It would be our only chance as we would be leaving early in the morning for Genoa. We hired an open carriage and set off to the accompaniment of the sound of hooves on cobbles. It was an eerie excursion lit by a bright moon, full of shadows and dark shapes which the street lamps did little to dissipate, and then suddenly, round the angle of a building, the ethereal majesty of the cathedral burst upon us. For a long time afterwards I found it difficult to realise that it did actually exist; we drove slowly

Itala car at Genoa 1914. Joseph Conrad and Mrs Conrad in the back with John between them

past without stopping and I had the feeling that somebody was playing a trick on me. The whole building seemed to glow with a light coming through the fabric which in some extraordinary way made it appear to be ghostly as well as majestic. It was more like a phantasy of the mind than a tangible object built by man. No photograph can convey the beauty it possesses when seen by the light of the moon.

Next morning we left for Genoa where my father managed to get us a passage on a Dutch steamer which would be sailing in a few days. To help fill in the time my father arranged for us to visit the grottoes near the town. I remember very little about them, except some rather rough stonework and intensely blue water, and the reason for that was the drive from the hotel – by far the most frightening journey I have ever made. The road wriggled up the side of a steep hill, hairpin bends following one another in rapid succession with a wall of rock on one side and an unfenced drop of hundreds of feet on the other. The driver of the car, an Itala, was firmly of the opinion that he was in competition with all the other drivers to get to the top in the shortest possible time. My father sitting beside him kept telling him to slow down but he shrugged his shoulders, let go of the wheel and waved his hands to explain that it was quite safe, then grabbed it again just in time to steer round the next hairpin. My mother was the most phlegmatic of people, nothing seemed to ruffle her, but that journey did disturb her equilibrium. My father gave the driver a real dressing down, explaining that we wanted to look at the grottoes from this earth and not from the heavens. When it was time to return we were all a bit apprehensive but my father's comments had been taken to heart and we descended at a much more moderate speed – perhaps the threatened loss of a tip had something to do with it.

We boarded the steamer and after we had stowed our belongings in our cabins I was allowed to have a run on deck. I had emerged on the port side, gone forward under the bridge and had reached the after end of the upperdeck, when I saw a man asleep on the canvas cover of a loaded barge about fifty feet away. He was lying on a tightly stretched tarpaulin and looked to me in a very precarious position. I hung around waiting to see if he would slip into the water. My father came and stood beside me as preparations were made to cast off and I pointed out the sleeping man. A motor boat came between our steamer and the barge creating quite a wash, enough to disturb the barge and the sleeper, who slid gracefully into the water feet first, very quietly. The men on the dockside were not aware of their friend's fate until they heard the splashings and the flow of imprecations. When we saw that he could swim we joined in their laughter, my father remarking that it was as well that I did not understand Italian. After their mirth had subsided they pulled him out and chaffed him for sleeping at the wrong time of the day.

There was not a lot to remember of the voyage home as the steamer was a cargo vessel with only a few passengers and watching the sea go by day after day was not an exciting pastime. As we approached Gibraltar a British destroyer came out and steamed alongside, inspected our papers and with a flurry of foam astern disappeared back to harbour. We did not call at the Rock and could see nothing of interest as we steamed through the Straits.

Only one incident comes to mind of that trip and it was at dinner one evening as we crossed the Bay of Biscay. The steward, in a vain attempt to save himself from falling, poured a plateful of soup over my mother's lap. JC let fly and was far from complimentary as the wretched man made himself scarce.

We proceeded up the Channel, rounded the north foreland and steamed up London's river to dock at Tilbury, but how we made the rest of the journey back to Capel House I have no idea. So ended our trip to Poland of which I remember so little due to being ill, or at any rate, not too well, so I have been told. My father seems to have been fated to be unlucky in his efforts to take us for holidays outside the British Isles.

Capel House, 1914–19

The boy. First lessons – no hobbies – Mrs C's lack
of interest – friends in uniform – prehistoric animals
– Colvins – Wedgwoods – Maskelyne and Devant –
Pinker – lunching out – Jane Anderson – first
bicycle – circuses – school – ticking off

Soon after we got back from Poland we settled into the way of life we
had enjoyed before, and although the war made changes they were
gradual and I hardly noticed them. It had very little impact on my
life at the time as I was too young to appreciate the news and my
parents kept what there was of it to themselves. My brother was not
yet old enough to join up but seemed to spend a lot of time away from
home rather to my mother's chagrin. He was nine years older than
me and we were never very close and, I confess, I was only vaguely
aware of his absences.

Before we went to Poland I had had elementary lessons from my
aunt, Nellie George, as she was then, and I was able to read and
write, so long as one ignored the ink splodges. My mother hoped that
her sister could come and stay and so be a companion to her and
teach me. However my grandmother's poor health prevented this
hope from being achieved. My parents decided, or rather my mother
decided and my father appeared to agree, that I should not be sent
away to school until after my ninth birthday. It was arranged with
Mr Farrer, headmaster of the local village school, that I should have
an hour's tuition at five in the afternoon for five days each week.
Before the lessons started my father explained to me the necessity of
learning and the importance of listening to what I was told. It was
not long before I got over my initial shyness and I came to look
forward to the visits, often extended over the hour to explain something or answer a question.

My father never had any hobbies; he did not collect stamps, or
butterflies, or antiques, nor did he make anything such as toys or
simple furniture. In those days very few people seemed to have
hobbies though some did admit to having an interest in acquiring

brass or silverware, or in huntin', shootin', and fishin', none of these had any attraction for my father. If asked what his hobbies were he would put his eyeglass to his eye, examine his questioner closely, and say that his time was fully occupied with his work and his books. If that reply elicited the question, 'Do you buy specially bound editions?' He would say he bought books to read, not to stare at their backs on a shelf while they collected dust over the years. He liked books to be well bound but it was their contents that mattered and he never kept a book of which he did not approve – there was no room for 'bosh' in his bookcases. He was a fast reader, not a skimmer reading bits here and there, but a perspicacious reader who obtained the greatest satisfaction from a good story well written.

After our return from Poland my father seemed to take a greater interest in my activities and this could well be so as my mother was definitely becoming more crippled and the pain in her knee getting worse. He took more interest in my toy cars of which I had a really wonderful collection, nearly all of them given to me by him. All had some form of steering and either clockwork motors or heavy lead flywheels which one wound up to a high speed with the handle provided. He would help me lay out books on the floor to represent roadways with side turnings and then he would time me while I carried out various manoeuvres under his instructions.

I have referred before to my 'ships' and I think my father found talking about them rather a relief during the tension of these days. We used to have long conversations about them at meal-times. He knew most of my ships by name and it was remarkable to me how he remembered their peculiarities from our previous conversations and would haul me up short if I contradicted myself about cargoes or destinations.

'You said that *The Glowworm* was bound for Singapore with a cargo of coal so she cannot be loading pig-iron at Cardiff', or '*The Grasshopper* should berth tomorrow at high tide, that will make about a hundred and twenty days from Adelaide, a fair passage.' My mother would get very tired of these imaginings and she would say so, complaining that she had two toddlers to look after as well as all the other jobs, at which JC would silence me with a look and glare at her.

Looking back at the sudden stops in these conversations, it seems to me that my father was trying to take us out of ourselves and did not realise that my mother had not kept with us. I think this happened fairly often when the subject under discussion had no interest for her.

After all, my ships and cars were no part of her world, which was understandable, and apart from injunctions not to fall in the water or get in her way when playing with a car they might not have existed at all for her. She was always busy typing, sewing, cooking and only very seldom did she ever take a break until after dinner in the evening. If I was ill in bed she would make time to read me a story, but, actually, sewing and crochet-work were her chief relaxations though I often had the impression that they were being done against the clock.

Most of our friends were doing war work of one kind or another; Cunninghame Graham had gone off to South America to buy horses for the British government, Percival Gibbon had gone as a war correspondent on the Western front and Richard Curle was doing his bit in the air force. It was only very rarely that one of them could come to visit us. They would arrive, in uniform, be given a meal, talk with my parents for an hour or so and then depart. JC and my mother were always glad to see anyone and heartened by the visit, but, when the visitor had gone, a shadow seemed to pass over the house and my parents would become silent, lost in their own thoughts. I was conscious of these changes without being fully aware of the reason for them at the time. It was not until much later that I realised that the shadow was due to their anxiety for my brother or sometimes for a friend who had called in on his way to rejoin his unit at the front.

So the weeks and months passed by and my mother became more crippled with her damaged knee, my father writing, with occasional periods in bed with gout, and myself being more or less good and not getting into mischief too often. I was well provided with toys and having been brought up to find my own amusement I could always find something to do. I was learning more from my lessons and took more interest in books, particularly those which my father read to me or I read to him. I soon learnt not to guess at words. My father did not approve of words being 'made a mess of' and would stop me until I had sorted the words out, explaining that they were to be treated with care, like friends. Treated properly they were good friends but if one abused them they could become enemies.

He often spent an hour or so in the evening showing me pictures in Hutchinson's *Creatures of other days*, describing how the artist had built up the picture from pieces of bones of prehistoric animals; or he would read to me about far away places, explaining how the natives built their houses on poles driven into the river beds of eastern rivers. He would enjoy telling me about these things until someone came into the room, when he would stop abruptly. It did not matter who came in, my mother or the maid, he very rarely continued his conversation at that time. Very occasionally he would pick up the thread of the story several days later, especially if it concerned some episode in which he had taken part.

When we went to London we stayed at the Norfolk Hotel in Surrey Street which was convenient for my father to visit his literary agent, J. B. Pinker. I enjoyed these trips to London when we visited our friends, Sir Sidney and Lady Colvin, Ralph Wedgwood, Will Rothenstein, Cunninghame Graham and Richard Curle. The Colvins were very old friends of ours and they always made me welcome, providing me with some massive volume with numerous illustrations while they talked with my parents. Sometimes I would listen to their conversation but I must have been listening with 'half an ear' as JC said because I do not remember anything about them. At other times I would accompany my mother up the flight of shallow stairs to the rather dimly-lit drawing room on the first floor. It was a long room going from back to front of the house, full of furniture, little glass-topped tables with spindly legs filled with a variety of *objets d'art* which made me a bit nervous in case I knocked something over. Later on when we took our maid with us I would be sent on in her care, after we had deposited my parents with the Colvins, to Mr Lorberg's shop in Kensington High Street, where I'd spend the money JC had given me on a toy or a model.

It was Richard Curle who introduced my father to Ralph Wedgwood, who was knighted later on, and who became a close friend of my father. We must have visited their house in Sheffield Terrace fairly often when we were in town but I only remember one evening in particular. We had been to dinner and afterwards Ralph Wedgwood's son, John, and his daughter, Veronica, took me off to their playroom in the basement to entertain me. I think I may have been rather 'small fry' for them but I remember pushing a model railway engine, making 'chuff-chuff' noises along a length of track laid on the floor and hearing John Wedgwood's voice above me saying, 'You need not do that. It has its own exhaust.' It was a two-and-a-half-inch-gauge working model of an Atlantic passenger engine with 4–4–2 wheel arrangement and I really ought to have crept into the first hole or crevice I could find but instead I thanked him

for telling me. He laughed and said I had the cheek of the
devil.

It became a regular part of our visit to London for my parents to
take me to see Maskelyne and Devant's Mystery Show at St George's
Hall. We usually sat three or four rows back from the stage and on
one occasion Maskelyne asked for somebody to go up on the stage to
help him with his next trick. My father nudged me and said, 'Go on,
up you go'. I felt very self conscious, dressed in a sailor suit which I
disliked but which was my usual attire on these occasions. I made my
way up the steps leading to the stage to be met at the top by Mr
Maskelyne. He patted my chest and said, 'Good gracious! What
have you got here?' and pulled out a string of sausages. He then felt
under the collar of my sailor's suit and produced something else. I
was getting more and more perturbed and getting nearer and nearer
to the point of dashing off the stage when I heard JC laugh and clap
his hands and realised that I must not let him down. I do not
remember what the trick was that Maskelyne performed but
whenever I am called upon to stand up in public to talk to people I
always recall with gratitude the memory of Jasper Maskelyne for
getting me over those first few moments of my first public appearance. I will not say I am not nervous when I stand up in public; I
think most people are, but it never seems as bad as that first time at
St George's Hall.

A frequent visitor to the hotel when we were in town was J. B.
Pinker who, as my father's literary agent, did a great deal for him for
which I am extremely grateful. JB, as he was always known, was a
very understanding and shrewd friend and often came to see us at
Capel House and later at Oswalds. He never became a close friend of
mine although I met him often in London. It was only a short walk to
his office in Arundel Street and my father would call and ask me to
take some manuscript or a note across to him. I would take the lift up
to the firm's office and be ushered into his room where he sat behind
a large desk set across the corner so that the light came over his left
shoulder. He always had a smile and a friendly handshake for me
and if I had to wait for an answer he would provide me with an
illustrated weekly – The Tatler or The London News. Then he would
return to his chair, remove his spectacles, hold them up to the light
and give them a polish with his handkerchief before starting to read
whatever it was that JC had sent him. It was very quiet in his room
and one could only just hear the traffic in the street below; the only

noise that broke the silence was a series of short bursts of sound like water dripping from a tap, just loud enough to attract attention. I did not want to appear rude and stare at him but the noise was coming from Pinker himself. By turning my chair, ostensibly to get better light on my magazine, I could watch his reflection in the window apparently without him being aware. He appeared to read a sentence or a paragraph from the paper he was holding, then raise his head as though looking at the ceiling but with his eyes closed and, as he did so, his lips moved just enough to make the noise of water dripping. The amount of noise seemed to be directly related to the intensity of his thoughts though I am sure that it was an entirely subconscious action, sometimes there was only one 'drip' and at others a whole 'string of drips' which would continue for quite a while. I have written elsewhere that the books of Beatrix Potter formed a large part of my early reading and often I found myself thinking of Pigling Bland while I waited. Pinker had a fresh complexion; rather pink and white, and this, coupled with his neat and tidy attire, must have encouraged these thoughts since there was no other reason for the association of ideas.

He did a great deal for my father quite apart from the financial assistance he gave in the early years, though his motives were not entirely altruistic as he admitted to me on one occasion. I had taken a batch of papers to him and had waited while he made a telephone call concerning them. When he had finished the conversation, to which he had bid me listen, he said to me, 'Well, you heard all that so you can tell your father. Tell him I will write and confirm the arrangement in a day or two. You do realise that I am acting for your father but I shall also benefit by the proposition. That is business.' Apart from this one time he never commented on or explained anything of his association with my father and it was only many years later that I realised just how much he had helped my father by providing both financial and moral support before JC achieved fame.

He was about the same height as my father and wore similar clothes, dark suits, white shirts with stiff stand-up collars. However, while JC looked distinguished, Pinker looked well-dressed – perhaps a bit over-dressed in his business rig of frockcoat and grey striped trousers. The first time I saw him dressed in this way I put my foot in it by asking my mother, in a stage whisper, what tricks he was going to do; I had only seen magicians wearing clothes like that before.

He came to my father's rescue when JC's bank failed and at other times when the financial tide had ebbed a bit more quickly than was expected. Through the years he became a very close friend and trusted adviser in whom my father had complete confidence right up to the time of his death in America in 1922. He built the literary agency into a prosperous firm in spite of unkind criticism on the part of some people to whom he was not as generous as he was to my father. I think it may have been for that reason that he was not as popular with JC's other friends and I do not recall ever seeing him at one of my mother's 'tea-fights' which she used to arrange when we were in town.

After JB's death his eldest son took over the running of the American office while the younger one managed the London office. With JB gone, my father had not the same confidence in the management and several times I heard him discuss with Richard Curle the possibility of making a change. After the American office got into difficulties Curle wrote to me advising me to get in touch with my co-trustee and take the literary estate to another agent. Unfortunately the collapse of the London office occurred before we could make other arrangements and we, along with many others, suffered considerable financial loss. It was several years before J. M. Dent and Sons, who took over the management of the literary estate, could restore confidence and disentangle the muddles that had been created by Pinker's office. Still, as JC would have said, 'that's all water under the keel'.

It is ironic that JC, who was so punctilious about fair dealing in business and day-to-day dealings, should have been caught in two financial failures. I remember one morning returning from a shopping expedition to Canterbury when he had given me some money to buy something for him. I put the parcel and the change on his desk, (I always kept any change from these commissions in a separate pocket). He opened the parcel and looked at the bill, then at the money I had put down, then turned his gaze on me.

'They have given you ten shillings too much, haven't they?'

'Yes, so you are ten shillings to the good.'

'That is not the point. It is dishonest. If you knew that they had given you too much you should have handed it back there and then. Now you can get on your bicycle and ride back to Canterbury, take this ten shilling note and explain.'

I pointed out that there was not much time to go there and back before lunch, to which JC replied: 'There is just time to prove that you are honest. How can you complain if you are overcharged if you do not do so when you are undercharged, eh? Remember that in future.'

When we were in London numerous friends would drop in for tea and quite often there would be a dozen or more talking to my parents or among themselves. On these occasions I was expected to be in attendance looking after the guests, seeing that they had all that they needed, tea, food and cigarettes. They were all easy to talk to and did not seem to be bored with my rather limited number of topics of conversation – I found young people of my own age far more difficult to converse with and it took a number of meetings before my shyness wore off. I was always aware but not really surprised that my father did not interrupt me if I was talking to a friend, he would listen for a short while before joining in. He had impressed upon me that it was bad manners to barge in on a conversation and he was always most scrupulous about behaving correctly and really did practise what he preached.

My parents enjoyed lunching at various restaurants when in town and were often invited by our friends to certain of them, the choice being limited (by my mother's lameness) to those without stairs to the dining room. One day we had been invited to a well-known restaurant in Regent Street. My father and I had lagged rather a long way behind the rest of the party so to save time he took off his coat and hat as he walked in, handed them to a very resplendent person with lots of gold ribbons and buttons on his uniform saying, 'Take these, my good man', and went on after the others.

Meanwhile as I was struggling out of my coat the man came across to me and said, with a strong American accent, 'Was that Joseph Conrad?'

I replied, 'Yes it was.'

With a broad grin he said, 'Most likely I am the first American officer that Joseph Conrad has given his hat and coat to then!'

Visits to 13 Airlie Gardens, where the Rothenstein's lived, were always enjoyed by us though I am afraid that John and his sister Betty, found me rather dull and gauche. This was not intentional but was because I spent so much time on my own at Capel and was lost when I met children of my own age in London. I was happy, but my world was my model ships, and cars – an inanimate world in which there was no interaction or conversation, and the only person who

John, Jane Anderson, Mrs Conrad and Joseph Conrad in the garden at Capel House

took any interest was my father. I tried to get my mother to take notice but her response was, 'Not now dear, some other time', but the 'other time' never came. I know I was much better off than my father had been at my age but I can remember longing for someone to play with, when I stopped to think about it. A couple of boys from the village were asked up but the afternoon ended in their fighting and smashing furniture.

It was during the war that Jane Anderson came to interview my father for an American publication and before long she was a regular visitor. My father was always very courteous to females in all walks of life and pretty ones in particular. Sometimes his courtesy was misinterpreted, depending on the upbringing of the lady concerned, but in the case of Jane Anderson it did not appear to me that she took advantage of my father's behaviour though I am bound to admit that my mother was jealous of her to some extent. She was good looking and had a good figure and was always well and neatly dressed. She was one of the very few women, young and unattached, who came to see us at Capel House. She was vivacious and not against having a mild scrap with me, rolling me on the floor while my father looked on with amusement. All the other women who came were married, some rather staid and practically everyone of them nervous and on their best behaviour. I noticed that my father's rather foreign way of bringing his heels together, bowing from the hips and kissing the back of their hands seemed to upset their equilibrium and some went so far as to snatch their hand away as though they had been stung. I was always curious to see their reactions, which varied a lot, especially with people living round about – some smiled, others looked surprised, and several blushed. I remember once when a padre from a neighbouring parish called with his good lady. JC as usual started to raise her hand to his lips when the padre knocked it away saying, 'We do not do that sort of thing in this country!' JC looked surprised, then gazed at him for a short while and said, 'No, of course not. Now I come to look closely you have difficulty in finding your mouth, to judge by your clothes! Good afternoon', turned on his heel and retired to his room, slamming the door. The padre had not bothered to make himself presentable and his vestment was liberally stained with food, while his hands would have benefited from soap and water. Subsequent enquiries revealed that the padre was a passionate gardener who devoted more time to his hobby than to his job.

On one visit Jane Anderson asked my parents if they would let me take her for a bicycle ride, saying she had asked the housemaid to lend her machine if there was no objection. Although my mother was not very pleased with the idea she agreed when my father approved and warned Jane that he did not know my 'ability as a pilot' and then turned to me to ask what route I proposed taking. I replied that we would go down to Hamstreet, up to Warehorne, turn right and come back through the woods past Burnt Oak Cottage. It was a sunny day with a strong westerly wind blowing when we left after lunch. Although she had ridden a bicycle before it took Jane a little while to find her balance and there were one or two hectic wobbles and swerves before we turned left at the Sugarloaf corner onto the main road to Hamstreet. We negotiated the hill down into the village where Jane insisted that we must buy some sweets at Mrs Godden's shop. After making our purchases we turned back towards the post office where we turned left along past the old cottages, under the railway and up the short steep little hill and over the brow before the gentle slope down to cross the ditch by Burr Farm. When we were over the top of the hill Jane suggested that we should race for the corner.

We were pedalling furiously down the slight incline when I heard her exclaim, which made me look round. 'You should not look round when that happens!', the wind had caught her skirt and had blown it well above her knees.

'Oh, why not? I think your legs are very beautiful!'

That was nearly the end of the ride, for in her anxiety to pull her skirt down she nearly wobbled into me. However, we turned the corner and with the wind behind us returned home without mishap. She described the trip to my father and told him of my remark at which he laughed, observing 'that it is well to start making compliments early in life because later it becomes more difficult, and one should practise at all times'.

Talking of bicycles reminds me of how I obtained my first machine by what can only be called an accident. I had been playing by the moat and had come across a number of underwater obstructions, so had decided to dredge the channels to make a better way through for my ships. As I dredged, a very old and rusty bicycle frame came up on the end of the cable which I was using to pull out the branches and other rubbish. As I hauled it up the bank it occurred to me that I might be able to do something with it. Anyhow I left it to dry and continued my dredging further along the moat, where, after a while, I brought up an old wheel, somewhat rusty but still a wheel. A few days later, poking around in one of the sheds, I found another wheel. Two wheels and a frame! The wheels were of different sizes but that did not matter. All I needed was a pair of handlebars as the old frame still had the front forks attached and with generous quantities of oil and some brute force they were made to turn again. I found the handlebars in the ashes of a bonfire at the back of the oast-house and with much labour and effort I managed to straighten them and fit them to the frame; after further struggling the wheels were in their respective positions. After a few awe inspiring tumbles I managed to stay on the contraption and roll down the slope and across the north moat and a little way up the rise to the oast-house, where I turned round and repeated the exercise in the opposite direction. It was not long before JC got to know of my escapade and came out to watch me. He realised how dangerous it was, with no tyres or saddle, no brakes or pedals. I only stayed on by putting my foot on the tube where the pedal shaft should have been. He watched me do an 'out and back' trip and then said, 'You put that damned contraption away and I will give you a bicycle'. Needless to say the contraption was dumped on the rubbish heap forthwith and a few days later I saw the gardener wheeling it down the drive on his way to 'lose it'. JC made a special trip into Ashford and a few days afterwards the carrier brought a brand new Humber bicycle in the afternoon. I rushed in to thank JC and tell him that it had arrived. He came to look at it and then patted me on the shoulder and said, 'Come, get on and ride it.' This was rather a tall order as I had only ridden the 'cantankerous contraption' previously and the new bicycle was a very different proposition. However, after about ten minutes I managed to get away from the person who had been steadying me and from then on I had no difficulty.

My father thought of all sorts of exercises for me to do; a sort of slalom course weaving between thin sticks set about six feet apart down the centre of a narrow path, and a 'slow' race round the flower beds when I had to take as long as possible to complete the course without turning back or putting my feet on the ground. JC never rode a bicycle though he thoroughly enjoyed the 'trick' cyclists at circuses and I was always taken to at least one performance if there was a circus within reasonable distance. He had very definite preferences for some acts and he did not really approve of making lions, tigers and bears perform, he thought that it was beneath their dignity. Horses, elephants, seals and monkeys he enjoyed watching but acrobatic and trapeze artists were not so interesting though he enjoyed the tight-tope artists. I think that his favourite acts were juggling and sleight of hand, with trick cycling and balancing close alternatives. When we had returned home after a visit to a circus he would join me in the garden to walk along a pole supported clear of the ground on piles of bricks, and he was very good at keeping his balance but he maintained that it was easier to walk along a pole than a rope.

Towards the end of the spring of 1915 my parents decided after much discussion, that I should go as a weekly boarder to a school in Ashford. My father did not like the idea but gave way to my mother's wishes and so for a few weeks I suffered the intense unhappiness of homesickness. JC realised that I would not settle down at this particular school where my companions had such a different outlook and with whom I could find no common ground; so after a few weeks I was kept at home while my father cast around to find a more suitable school. Eventually he decided to send me to Ripley Court in Surrey where, in spite of my mother's protests, I would be far enough away to preclude any daily or weekly visits and thus was confident that I would get over my homesickness more quickly.

Mrs Pearce, who owned the school, ran it with the help of Mr Church and between them they managed to reassure my mother sufficiently for her to agree that I should be left with them at the beginning of the autumn term. I was homesick but as the school kept every one of the boys fully occupied we were all tired at bed time and fell asleep before any memories could come flooding in. In a very short time I began to enjoy school life and settled in fairly well though I did not make any lasting friendships. Looking back I am rather glad that I was brought up to find my own amusements and the time I spent with my father, which probably amounted to minutes each day was so charged with interest that it did me more good than hours spent in any other person's company.

Mrs Pearce and Mr Church were considerate and thoughtful people who did all they could to make life tolerable and I responded to their efforts in most subjects but I just could not find any enthusiasm for Latin. Often I was asked how I thought my father could write such good English if he had not learnt Latin, completely overlooking the fact that he would have been taught it by a Polish tutor. I would reply that my father learnt English 'before the mast' in the collier brigs of the east coast and from the local newspapers. They would smile knowingly and appear to accept my answer, though with some scepticism. I was vaguely worried that people did not accept my answer as I did not realise what the language of the fo'c'sle could be like, and without being unkind, I doubt very much if they did either. Some of the comments made in front of me very soon made me aware that very few of them had the sort of imagination or capacity for making a fair judgement.

The question, answer and disbelief continued to recur from time to time and I asked my father why it was that people seemed reluctant to accept the truth, which was what it was to me. He gave very careful thought to his reply which was perhaps a little over my head though, as I grew up, I understood it better. In his opinion it was partly due to the lack of imagination of some people and partly to the idea, strange to us, that because they had not learnt a foreign language they thought that my father was some sort of freak for being able to do so. There was also the bias against the eastern European which made it hard for them to accept that his earliest contact with spoken English was in the fo'c'sles of the *Mavis* and *The Skimmer of the Seas*. Few of them had the imagination or the ability to create any sort of picture of the day-to-day existence in those circumstances of which they knew little or nothing and probably cared less.

Then there were the people, few in number among our acquaintances, who tended to look down on newspaper correspondents as though they were inferior beings and incapable of writing such English as would help to educate a foreign seaman to speak, let alone write, readable English. As one of them remarked, 'Don't see how he can write English if he hasn't been to "Varsity".' My father had a very high opinion of the correspondents of those days who wrote well and took a pride in their work, and often referred affectionately to 'those men of the East Coast papers who, unknowingly, tutored my early days in England'. At that time, the idea of a foreign seaman being able to learn English 'before the mast' and from the newspapers was extraordinary, as was the quality and style of his writing when considered against the background of the somewhat limited vocabulary of the men with whom he sailed. Few could spell his name, let alone pronounce it, and in addition there was the characteristic reticence of the English towards foreigners. JC claimed, with justification, that he knew the two ends of the language, the rough and the smooth, and that he was able to appreciate it better coming from abroad as he could 'see' the language so much more clearly than those brought up 'within it'. He referred to the language of the fo'c'sle as being picturesque but I cannot recall a single occasion of his using any picturesque vernacular. He would not allow any profanity in his hearing and only swore under provocation; usually 'damn and blast' or 'Donner und Blitzen' and one or two French expressions, which relieved his annoyance.

He never swore at anyone when he gave them a dressing-down and if he did say 'and don't be such a damned fool another time', it was not said with any aggression. He was always very fair when he gave one a 'ticking off' and listened to the culprit's explanation before expressing himself. He had a knack of making one feel very small for misdemeanours without raising his voice or indulging in any swearing. I know because I got into mischief several times and was made to feel exceedingly small. Whenever he had cause to 'tick off' any member of the staff he did so alone with the culprit, never in front of anyone else, and, if possible, the reprimand was given at the time of the misdemeanour.

Spring Grove and Oswalds, 1919–24

The youth. JC visits the navy – 'Q' ships – air-raid
– Mrs C's knee – Sir Robert Jones – brother gassed
– half-term lunch – Nellie Lyons – Spring Grove –
looking for a car – operation in Liverpool – back to
Ripley Court – driving lessons

The war dragged on but it did not have any impact to speak of on me
as my parents did not discuss it when I was about. If I asked a
question about the war my father answered it briefly, but my mother
would either ignore the question or say that it did not concern me.
For most of the time I was at preparatory school but on several
occasions I was called home to keep my mother company if JC had to
be away, and so it was in early November of 1916 that I returned
home to be with my mother.

My father had been asked by the Admiralty to visit some units of
the Royal Navy so his wish to do something to help was at last
fulfilled. He had said, very often, that he wished he could do something, however insignificant, so it gave him considerable pleasure
when the letter arrived. He tried not to show his eagerness as my
mother was more than a little anxious about this trip. There had
been quite animated conversation between them that I had not
followed, and after I had helped my mother with the washing-up she
went into the drawing room and continued the conversation. I
stayed up quite late that evening after returning from school, I
remember, and had not gone to sleep when they came upstairs.
Usually I had dropped off by the time my mother came up, after
listening to the murmur of voices in the drawing room below. My
father used to work late into the night or more correctly into the early
morning, coming to bed about half past two or three o'clock. I heard
them talking through the open doorway between our rooms while my
mother did the packing for JC. There was a pause and then my
mother said, 'Boy, don't go – you know I wish you weren't going!
What shall I do if anything happens?'

'Come, come, Jess, I can't back out now even if I wanted to. You must realise that and besides you know and have known all along that I have set my heart on this trip or something like it. I'll be alright, you'll see. There is nothing to worry about and you have Jackilo to keep you company. He'll see you are alright. You just carry on till I come aboard again.'

The day arrived when he was due to leave and as he put his coat on he turned to me and said, 'Oh, lend me that gold pencil please, the one given you recently. I must have something to write with.' I rushed off to get it. It had not yet become a precious possession and I was very pleased that my father should have asked me to lend him something of mine. We saw him out to the taxi and, after he had kissed my mother goodbye, she said with a very straight face: 'Mind you don't get your feet wet!' My father turned back and said with equal seriousness: 'Seagulls always do when they alight on the sea!' We were all in a state of tension but my parents felt more than I did. Although I was aware of my mother's anxiety I was also conscious of a feeling of pride at, and a sympathy for, my father's eagerness to be off and away. We stood and watched the taxi go down the drive and disappear behind the hedge and as we waved the tension evaporated to be replaced by a feeling of loneliness which all the efforts of Nellie Lyons, our maid, could do nothing to dispel.

With my father away Capel seemed to become very empty and my mother found the solitude too much of a burden with only the household and a small boy to talk to, so she decided to go to Folkestone and stay at the Royal Pavilion Hotel down by the harbour. We managed to get rooms on the first floor in the eastern corner overlooking the quays and the channel. My recollections of this period are very vague, except for the tedious walks along the Leas or the shore with Nellie Lyons while my mother talked with the other people staying in the hotel. After what seemed to me to be a long time we heard from my father and returned to Capel House to wait for him.

I remember being wakened late in the night, or perhaps, the early hours of the morning, by JC bending over my bed to greet me, his shadow, cast by the light of a candle, seemed immense and grotesque as it passed over the ceiling. The excitement of the trip and the long journey home from the north had made him rather tired and it was some days before we heard the salient points. I had the impression that he spoke more from a desire to 'fill the silence', as my mother did not seem to have any interest in his adventure, than to tell us what had happened.

He was most apologetic for having dropped my pencil overboard into the North Sea when he was taken for a flight in a Short seaplane but said he would get another like it when he went to town. Gradually we heard more about his adventures but what pleased him above everything else was the kindness and appreciation shown him by the officers and men of the Royal Navy.

He had been to sea in a 'Q' ship for about ten days, hunting for German submarines, which he thoroughly enjoyed as the sea air and excitement made him feel much fitter. Later on he explained to me with the help of sketches, how the dummy deck cargoes folded down to expose the guns with which the ships were armed. After a number of explanations he asked me to build him a model, complete with dummy cargoes and guns, out of Meccano. This time I took care to sheet over the metal structure with cardboard, remembering the doubts he expressed previously about the seaworthiness of ships built of metal strips with holes in! He was delighted when I carried the model into his room and showed him how it operated, and it stayed on a table in his room when I returned to school. In the holidays he would ask me to 'Send an artificer to adjust the catches' or carry out other minor repairs. It never occurred to me that some people might think that he was selfish in retaining the model; in fact I was rather flattered and proud that I had created something that gave him so much pleasure. I had plenty of other toys and occupations to keep me busy.

One evening the postman arrived in a great splutter asking if we had seen the German aircraft which he thought had been bombing the railway workshops at Ashford. We all trooped out into the garden and there, far above us, were six or seven Taubes, like little white 'bow-ties' coming from the direction of the town. I believe this was the first air-raid of the First World War but I do not remember seeing any other enemy aircraft though we saw several Zeppelins caught in the searchlights later on.

During the whole of this time my mother's knee had been getting steadily worse and more and more painful so that my father arranged for her to be seen by Sir Robert Jones. My mother had put on a lot of weight because she could not take any exercise and, for some unknown reason, no one suggested that she should go on a diet. She was very fond of rich cakes, and munched her way through numerous boxes of sweets, particularly chocolates, as well as drinking a fair quantity of spirits. I doubt very much whether she could have had the perseverance to have kept to a diet with constant pain in her leg. Sir Robert Jones saw her eventually and suggested that a St Thomas's splint might help to relieve the pain by taking some of her weight off the knee joint. Initially it gave some relief but it restricted my mother's movement even more and after about six months it was obvious that it was not having the effect that was hoped for and so we were told that an operation would have to be performed. This could not be done for some weeks and so my mother had to put up with the pain and wait and, as if this were not enough, she had the anxiety of my brother's war injuries, shell-shock and gas-poisoning in October of 1918.

I do not remember much of this period, it was an unhappy time and I suppose that it is only natural that those memories should be lost. My parents did not make a point of telling me about my brother's injuries and it was not until a long time afterwards that I found out. I was aware of my mother's lameness but living with it one rather took it for granted; not that I did not sympathise but there was nothing that I could do about it. She was a remarkably cheerful person though after so many years of pain she had become fragile and any asperity in my father's voice would induce a flood of tears or if she had been refused something she adopted a stubborn dumbness.

My schooling at Ripley continued with half-term visits by my parents which helped to break the monotony, and the feeling of remoteness which I was always àware of in term time. I would be taken out to lunch at the Talbot Hotel in the village, where various local people, advised of my father's presence by the 'bush telegraph', would stand round the bar casting surreptitious glances at our party. I don't know whether my parents were conscious of the interest as my father never gave any indication either by look or voice; but I was aware of it and rather at a loss to understand their behaviour. They were all people I saw each week, either at church or walking through the village, quite ordinary people retired from business or the forces. All, that is, except for one couple who had been 'out East' where the husband had been in the consular service, and who asked the master in charge of our 'walk' if they might have a word with me! They said that they were most anxious to meet my father and thought that I had behaved rather badly when I had not introduced them when they signalled me at the hotel. JC had warned me that he did not want to be introduced to anyone so I suggested that they should ask Mrs Pearce or the headmaster which upset them even more because they had already done so and had been advised to 'sheer off'. I learnt afterwards that it was partly a bit of social climbing and partly an attempt to engineer a meeting in order to win a bet.

On my mother's birthday 22 February 1919 the family descended on me for the regular half-term visit and brought with them Nellie Lyons, who had become one of the family by virtue of the many years she had spent with us. She had not much to say but I was glad to see her, though she looked even more unwell than ever: she had become very thin and suffered from the cold. During the previous holidays when we had been discussing nicknames she had suggested, in a pathetic way, that a good nickname for her would be 'Bones' or 'Never sweat'. This visit of hers to Ripley was the last time I saw her because soon afterwards she was taken to the hospital where she died. In earlier years my mother used to take her home, to the row of tiny cottages where the railway-men lived just to the north side of the railway station at Westenhanger, and where I would be given a piece of old Mrs Lyons's treacle toffee.

During March of that year the family moved to Spring Grove, Wye, which was rented furnished from Captain Halsey, RN the 'Invisible Halsey' as JC called him, since he never came to see us for the whole six months that we were there. The house was pleasant and well furnished but my father was not happy there and complained to me on several occasions that the 'other fellow' was watching him. I was there for the Easter and summer holidays of 1919 and I was quite conscious of what JC meant. There was a feeling that someone was watching one's every movement and this was not just induced by the fact that we had not got our own furniture. This was the first house in which JC had his own study, a bright and cheerful room which did not have to do double duty like the drawing room at Capel House.

The hall at Spring Grove was long and appeared narrow in spite of being about seven feet wide, with a square landing at the far end raised about six or seven inches above the rest. On the right the stairs rose towards the front door and on the left was the door to my father's study facing down the hall. An oriental rug lay on the highly polished boards of the landing between the step and the study door and several people had slipped on it when going upstairs but no one did anything to make it safer. The usual advice given was '—you'll get used to it being slippery—' or '—try to remember not to rush it too quickly'.

I had a couple of friends to stay, Robert Douglas and Cuthbert Tebb, sons of two of my father's friends and we played tricks on one another and got into various mischiefs. I forget what devilment I had perpetrated on them but they were after my scalp. I entered the hall at high speed and made for the stairs, trod on the rug, slipped and crashed stern first into the study door, sliding along on my back with my feet in the air coming to an abrupt halt with a resounding thud. Before I had time to get up – almost before the reverberations had faded away – the study door opened and JC looking over me away down the hall said, in a mild voice, 'Next time knock more quietly', and shut the door again. He never asked if I had hurt myself or if I had done any damage – he was just not interested, for which I was very grateful. I got up quietly, straightened the rug and made myself scarce, to be greeted by my friends with surprise. They had come in at the front door to see JC looking down the hall at them and felt sure that I would get a 'dressing-down'. I do not think that my father was aware of any of us and I took care not to tempt providence by asking him.

At this time we had a Studebaker open tourer, quite the most hair-raising car we ever had – its ability to skid at the least provocation was phenomenal and more than justified the nickname of 'Skidibeggar'. In fairness it should be said that its tyres were of different section, but in those days, provided that there was a tyre on each wheel, the shape was not considered important. We got it originally because it was very spacious and had ample room in the back for my mother who now used a stool on which to support her leg. It was not a satisfactory car and we had all taken a dislike to it so we had been casting around for another car. An advertisement had appeared in the local paper offering a Cadillac, in sound running order and good condition, for sale at Borough Green, near Wrotham. We arrived and asked at the post office where we would find the builder's yard at the address given in the paper, which turned out to be about a hundred yards west of the crossroads. We enquired at the office to be met by a blank stare and were then advised to ask 'Charlie' in the joiner's shop. He turned out to be an ancient carpenter with an amazingly fertile imagination. 'Wunerful car, got six wheels and eight cylinders, all made of copper with brass pipes and a hood!' When at last we managed to stem the tide of words we were told that the car was in the shed, 'under tarplins'; true, but the 'tarplins' were covered by all sorts of builder's junk and burst bags of cement. After about three-quarters of an hour the two men had exposed the front end and JC had got decidedly cross and refused to wait any longer saying 'I am not going to ride in what is left under all that rubbish!' So that was that and the search continued while I returned to Ripley for my last term there. After much searching they found another open tourer Cadillac, a 30 horse-power affair weighing about two tons, even more spacious than the 'Skidibeggar' which provided a smooth and luxurious ride, much to my mother's enjoyment.

My mother's regular letters had referred to the pain in her leg more often so I was not surprised when I was called into Mrs Pearce's study about the middle of November and told that I was to be sent home, as another operation would have to be performed on my mother's knee. So next day I was taken to London and put on the train for Canterbury, where I was met by Charles Vinten, our chauffeur, and deposited on the doorstep at Oswalds. I learnt that Sir Robert Jones was to make the knee joint rigid by 'dovetailing' the bones together in the hope that this would relieve the pain that my mother had put up with for so long. The operation would be a long one and, as it would require a good deal of attention afterwards, it was decided that it should be performed in Liverpool near Sir Robert's home.

Rooms were found for my father and myself and so all three of us boarded the train at Canterbury West which ran through to Liverpool without any changes being necessary, arriving at Lime Street in the evening. A car took us to the nursing home where we left my mother and JC and I proceeded on to our lodgings. The next day we visited my mother in the morning and again in the afternoon as the operation was to be carried out early the following day. My father and I spent an anxious morning and afternoon and later in the evening he went to see my mother for a short while. A day or so later I was taken in to see her and when JC had been reassured that she was making satisfactory progress I was sent back to school. (After several weeks my mother returned home but there was no lasting improvement in her leg and though the bones joined up there was no reduction in the pain.)

My father put me aboard the train for London in the early after-noon, under the watchful eye of a Scottish guard who assured him that he would take great care of the 'wee laddie'. As the evening light faded the guard took me along to the restaurant-car and I had tea by myself, in lonely state, feeling rather small but buoyed up by JC's parting words, 'I'm trusting you to take care of yourself for your mother's sake and mine.' Of course I'd take care, hadn't I seen him take his handkerchief from his pocket and blow his nose furiously, which I knew only too well was about the only display of feeling of which he was capable in public? It was my first long train journey alone and I was glad of the friendly attention of the guard who stopped and had a word with me when he passed. Then, as we ran into the outskirts of London, he took me along to the guard's van at the front, from where I watched the rain-swept streets glisten in the lamplights as they rotated past us. We rolled to a stop at the terminus and the guard, after telling me to wait, went in search of Mr Barnard. The admirable Barnard in whom my father had complete confidence, ran a fleet of hire-cars and had been telegraphed to meet me. The guard returned with him saying, 'Here ye are then, one wee laddie for schule. His Dad's a great mon, aye a great mon.' These last words were evoked no doubt by the generous tip my father had given him some two hundred miles before. My father always had a soft spot for Scotsmen, often telling me that they were the best engineers to have on steamers at sea, with east coast men on smaller sailing ships and Cornishmen on the larger ones.

It was with some misgivings that Mr Barnard let me sit beside him in front as it was a very wet and chilly evening and it was only by promising to let him know if I got cold that I was allowed to sit behind the enormous windscreen of the Renault limousine. After about half an hour he stopped and made me get into the back where he wrapped me in a rug before continuing the journey. When we arrived at Ripley Court he had quite a job waking me up as I had fallen asleep in the warmth of the rug. However, by dint of much shaking he eventually got me into the house where I was given a cup of cocoa and a biscuit before being sent up to bed.

At the end of term my brother came to fetch me in the Cadillac – what a car – four cylinders, each with a copper waterjacket, copper pipes with brass fittings, beautifully brazed joints and, refinement of refinements, an engine-driven two-cylinder tyre pump. In addition to the three-speed and reverse gearbox there were two crown wheels and pinions at the back axle, electromagnetically controlled, which provided two ratios so that in effect we had six forward speeds and two reverse. The gear-lever and handbrake were on the right, there was a wooden-rimmed steering wheel of large size and full weather protection, as well as a rear 'Auster' windscreen. Instead of a spare wheel it had a spare rim and tyre, held on to the wheel proper by eight specially shaped washers with captive nuts, quite satisfactory and safe provided they were properly seated and checked for tightness at regular intervals.

I remember that car with particular affection as it was the first real car that I drove. The first lesson came as a complete surprise when I heard my brother calling me to ask if I wanted to go with him and JC for a run. I was invited to get up in front which was unusual when my father was coming but I supposed that this was to be a special treat. We turned left out of Oswalds drive with my brother at the wheel, went up the hill to the main road, turned right towards Dover. After about two miles we turned left at Barham crossroads, up the hill and left again at the top towards Wingham where my brother pulled into the side and stopped. He got out of the car and as he walked round the front he signalled to me to get into the driving seat. By sitting well forward with a folded rug behind me I could just reach the pedals with the aid of the steering wheel. I had always taken an interest in the way people drove and knew fairly well how and when gears had to be changed and the years I spent in my pedal car at Capel had taught me quite a lot about steering. After a few brief instructions from my brother I was told to move off. Having set the hand-throttle to the right engine speed, I pushed the clutch out, engaged first gear, released the brake as I let in the clutch, accelerated and changed into second gear and then into top. I moved the hand-throttle to tick over speed and used the foot throttle. I felt rather small now that I was behind the wheel and I had my work cut out maintaining a steady course, the radiator cap would keep going from side to side! After being told to 'look ahead' several times I managed to ignore the radiator cap and steer a much straighter course. At this time, early in 1920, there was very little traffic on this road, an occasional horse and cart, a few bicycles and the odd car or two. We went past the pumping station then a bit further on, bearing left again down the lane to Bramling. The road here was narrow but there was no other traffic, then round the pub on the left, and a few yards further on we took the right turn for the Barham Downs and Bishopsbourne. After that I was often taken on the quiet roads for more driving lessons when my brother was at home. I was too young to get a driving licence but I got a lot of practice driving the car round to the front door, and as a special treat from the front door to the garage where I had to turn it round before reversing into the garage.

12

Oswalds – hedges – trees – the little people – noises in the roof – Milward – water under the floor – lighting plant

I had much to see and investigate during that first holiday at Oswalds. It was a very different house from Capel which was 'all of piece' and had not been the object of alterations and additions before our occupation. Oswalds existed as a 'small seat', according to Hasted, in 1800, but it had been 'Georgianised' and added to in the Victorian era by the addition of an immense billiard room. It had a certain grace and elegance about it but my father never felt at home in it and remarked to me several times that it was a 'machin à vivre'. My mother liked it and for her it was a much more suitable house; there were no massive thresholds at each doorway as there had been at Capel and the stairway of three short flights with landings at each turn allowed her to rest when going up or down stairs.

It was not a friendly house, it lacked the homeliness of Capel and was very much a 'residence' which unfortunately had not been taken care of by previous owners, with the result that it had acquired an air of faded gentility. The large sweep of gravel drive, enclosed by yew hedges, was separated from the narrow flower-bed along the front by a narrow strip of tired-looking grass. Well-established creepers were held by wire frames to the discoloured stucco of the wall and instead of making the house look 'mellow' made one think of it as a 'poor old house'.

Although our gardeners, Jack Burchett and Louis Ford, did their best to make a show of flowers along the front their efforts were spoilt by the showers of gravel thrown over the beds every time a car came to the front door. Elsewhere they had more success; the Dutch garden with its formal pattern of small flower beds each surrounded by dwarf box-hedges always delighted my father with its colour and tidiness, and the herbaceous border running down to the Nail

Jack Burchett and Louis Ford, gardeners at Oswalds

Bourne stream from the northeast corner of the house was a blaze of colour. This border could be seen over the yew hedge that lined the side of the path along this elevation, and several times I caught my father bending over to look along the top of the hedge to see that Louis Ford had clipped it true and even. The gardener was aware of JC's trick and left an occasional twig sticking up for my father to call his attention to. They knew that each was watching the other but neither would have admitted it. It was obvious to the two gardeners that my father had no interest in horticulture so the leaving of the odd twig could have been a sort of stimulant to make him take notice of their work. When all the clipping from the hedge cutting had been collected my father would take a stroll and inspect the work, making mental notes of any twigs or other items to which he would call their attention when the men were paid at the end of the week. JC often gave the impression, so I have since been told, that he was unaware of what work had been done and it was only when one got to know him well that one realised that there was very little indeed that escaped his notice. His approval or otherwise of the work done by the 'crew' was always justly assessed, praised or criticised as occasion demanded, but woe betide anyone who tried to 'pull a fast one' on him.

The view from the study window was divided by the stump of an old elm tree. To the left there was the prospect of the sloping grassland of Bourne Park with a shave of beech trees along the top bordering the Dover road. To the right of the elm one had a glimpse of the path through the 'wilderness' with beech, sycamore and ash trees, that led to the cottage by the Park gates where Burchett lived. In the spring the 'wilderness' was ablaze with daffodils among the trees, relieving the 'funereal' green of the yew hedges of which there were far too many. My father had a great liking for oak trees and complained that there were too few in the vicinity. I think his preference for 'auks', as he called them, was the association with ship-building. It was only very seldom that he would talk about trees and timber, though he had quite an extensive knowledge of the characteristics of various timbers used in shipbuilding.

Oswalds seemed to have more than its fair share of 'gremlins' and minor mishaps, not only to the property itself but to the people working there and to their possessions. Some were due to the lack of maintenance, others to thoughtless workmanship in the past, and some to the 'little people' as an Irish carpenter contended when he lost his lunchbox when repairing a fence. He came to the door and asked for a bit of bread and a glass of water but on JC's instructions was given a couple of 'man size' sandwiches and a bottle of beer. Later that afternoon I went to see how he was getting on, and after he had given me a message of thanks for my father he added: 'I'm sure the little people knew I'd get more than I lost when they took me lunchbox.' He was wrong as I found the remains of his box, which was cardboard, in the dog's kennel some days later.

The first incident was a banging in the roof over the window of my father's bedroom which occurred a short while before I returned from school. When I returned for the Easter holidays his first words were, almost before I'd got in the house,

'Jackilo, get something done to stop that damned banging, it keeps your mother awake.'

Arthur Foote, my father's valet/butler had found that the noise could be stopped by turning on a cold-water tap, and a procession of plumbers, 'specialists' and other experts had come, looked wise or vacant as was their habit, and achieved nothing. I went up to the attic floor after lunch but could not find anything wrong, so I asked the crew to let me know when it started and left it at that. Several days passed and then one evening when a bath was being run it started. I dropped what I was doing and rushed up to the cupboard where the tanks were, and saw how the noise was made. I found that I could stop the thumping by pressing on the end of the tanks, and that the noise ceased as the tanks filled up. It was Charles Vinten, our chauffeur, who suggested that I had a word with Mr Milward, the village blacksmith, to find out if he had any suggestions. He said he would come along as soon as we let him know that the noise had started. A few days later he was summoned and shown the offending tanks. After half an hour or so he came down and said that he would be back next morning. Just before midday he came down and asked me to tell my father that he had finished and would wait in the kitchen. I introduced JC to the blacksmith with whom he shook hands, asked him to sit down and told Foote to bring beer and glasses. Then, turning to Milward, he said:

'Now, tell me what you have done and why you think you have cured the trouble.'

Mr Milward explained that when the water level in the tank fell at the same time as a certain pump at the waterworks was being used, the pulsations in the waterpipe caused the ends of the tanks to 'pant' because the distance between them was the same as the 'pressure peaks' in the watermain. He had removed the straight pipe between the tanks and replaced it by a pipe with bends in it so that its length was 'out of phase' with the pump. We never had any more trouble during our stay at Oswalds.

This meeting between JC and Milward was the beginning of a friendship that developed over the years, a friendship based on the respect of one craftsman for the other, each was the master of his own trade and fully aware of the standards that each had set himself. The literature of the one was matched by the ironwork of the other. Often in the holidays my father would ask me to walk along with him to the forge after dinner, when Milward would see us approaching from his cottage and cross the road in time to clean the top of an anvil and place a sack on it for my father to sit on. They would talk about the middle east, European affairs, the lives of famous men, JC answering Luther Milward's questions and arguing in a friendly fashion on various topics. Sometimes Milward would talk about wrought-ironwork and occasionally make some little thing to explain a process or method of construction. Then it was,

'Get on they bellows, Mas' John, please, while I show your Dad what I mean.'

These demonstrations always delighted JC and he asked Milward to show me how to make leaves and scrolls and joints in wrought-iron. On a few occasions we would arrive when he was making a full-sized drawing on a sheet of iron with a chalk, and my father invariably asked permission to watch him at work, patiently waiting until Milward paused to listen to my father's request. Later, when I visited the forge by myself, Milward would remark on this saying that only a real artist would have the 'gumption' not to interrupt while someone was making a drawing. The three of us became good friends and I am eternally grateful for the advice and help Milward gave me on the many jobs we did together, wrought-iron gates, signs, railings and not least for the wrought-iron memorial panels he made as a tribute to my father.

I was told on my return from school that my father had complained now and again of hearing running water, usually making the remark after crossing the hall to his study. I was aware of an atmosphere of unease in the house and things were not made any better by my mother suggesting that JC had got some water in his ear and giving him a variety of instructions for getting rid of it.

Luther Milward

'You ought to sit in a chair, dear, with your head on one side and wag it!' was one of them, to which JC replied,

'Yes, Jessie, yes, quite, or hang by my feet from the landing. That would do just as well I have no doubt.'

One day after returning from Canterbury my father stamped his foot, which he often did when something was not to his liking. Luckily he was by a chair which he grabbed as the floor-boards broke and fell into the space below. When we had recovered from our surprise we noticed that there was the sound of flowing water coming from below the floor. There was a strong smell of fungus and rotten wood, and after pulling up some more flooring we could see that the water was coming in through the brickwork below the front door cill, trickling under the joists and disappearing through the foundation brickwork opposite. Temporary repairs were made until a new floor could be laid during which time we should have to go away. The stream through the garden began to dry up and so did the water under the floor. No one had any explanation for this underground stream; the owners were not interested, merely saying that it would be attended to with any other work that needed doing. I went along to the forge and discussed it with Milward, who told me that the stream that flowed along behind the forge and through the garden of Oswalds, had originally flowed along the side of the village street through the gateway to Oswalds and on under the front door, hall and passage and into the lake in Bourne Park. Sometime in the eighteenth century the stream had been moved over to its present position but whoever diverted it did not know or had ignored the fact that there was and still is an underground stream flowing below the visible 'Nailbourne'.

We did not have to wait long for the old adage that 'troubles come in threes' to come true and we were not really surprised after the 'noises in the roof', and collapse of the hall floor that the lighting plant would have to be overhauled and a new set of accumulators installed. As the sewage had to be pumped away by an electrically driven pump it meant we had to go away while it was being done. There was quite a bit of objection from our landlord at this and several rather acrimonious meetings took place before we got him to agree to get the work done while we went to stay at Deal.

13

Deal – Baker – seasickness – sailing – *Jeanette* –
Goodwins – Gull lightship – Scandinavian ship –
assumed toughness – wish to return to sea

It must have been the second or third week of the summer holidays
that saw us depart for the Southeastern Hotel at Deal, as it was then
called, which stood right on the front on the opposite corner to Deal
Castle. We clambered into the Cadillac, literally, one step up, onto
the running-board, then another over the high cill into the car; JC in
front by the chauffeur, Charles Vinten; Mrs C and I in the back,
stowed in with suitcases for which there was plenty of room. We went
across country through Barfreston, Eythorne and Great Mongeham,
and along the front to the hotel, where we had managed to get a suite
of rooms, two bedrooms and a sitting room on the southeast corner
on the first floor. There was an uninterrupted view from the north
foreland, along the whole length of the Downs to Hope Point at the
north end of the south foreland.

As dusk fell we sat in the glass porch and watched the flashing of
the signal lights of the lightships and lighthouses along the Channel.
I was surprised how well JC remembered the frequencies of the
various lights; by counting the flashes he could tell the South Goodwin, Cap Griz Nez, the Gull and further away the North Goodwin
light-vessel. As the minutes slipped by I waited for him to say
something of his life at sea, but nothing came.

In the morning we went for a walk along the front towards the
pier and I noticed one of the men, who looked after the pleasure
boats, looking very hard at JC. We were almost past the little cabin-
affair by which the man was standing when my father stopped, and
looked at the man with amazement slowly spreading over his face:
'Baker?'

'Yes, sir, after all these years. I've often thought of you and
whether I should let you know I was here.'

JC stood quite still for some moments repeating 'Baker', almost totally overcome, then he stepped forward and shook hands.

'Baker and I served on the *Riversdale* together.'

I shook hands as he said to JC 'Anyone would know he's your boy.' We spent most of the morning on Baker's pitch; they conversed in short bursts as they recalled the past but I did not listen – I did not know the people, the places or the atmosphere of which they spoke. I wandered away and had a look at the boats. There was a 'yawl-rigged' day boat which took my fancy as well as a number of 'gunter-rigged' dinghies and small rowing boats. Then I heard JC hail me to go back with him for lunch but not before he had arranged with Baker to be taken out that afternoon for a sail if the weather held. I think JC was aware that I was a bit apprehensive because there was quite a sea running with a stiff breeze from the south. Secretly I was hoping that the wind would drop. He pointed to a barge running before the wind, saying that there was just enough to fill the sail but she was a long way out, so I could not tell nor did I appreciate then that the white water at her bows was sea breaking on board.

After lunch JC took me down to the chandlers where we bought sou'westers, oilskins and long boots which came right over the knees, and then we headed back to Baker's pitch on the foreshore where he had a fourteen-foot centre-board dinghy ready for us on the 'slips'.

'Go on, get aboard.' I clambered over the gun'le to be followed by JC and Baker, 'Right, let her go!' And as the wave reached its peak we floated clear of the shingle. There seemed to be even more wind now that we were afloat and I only just heard JC shout:

'Get for'rd and heave on that halyard.' There was only one and after a bit I managed to get the spar fairly well up the mast. 'Swig on it and make fast.' What was all this? I hadn't any idea what he was talking about but Baker came to my rescue.

'Your first time in a small boat? You'll soon get the hang of it. Sit on the weather side and try to keep your body upright. You'll soon feel better.'

I tried to manage a smile but I was feeling the movement quite a bit and must have looked more than a little green. JC hauled in the sheet and we laid over on the starboard tack. That was better, just going up and down across the swell and I soon became comatose with the rhythm of the motion when suddenly, 'Stand by to go about.' Baker said, 'As the foot of the sail goes over move to the other side.' Then to JC, 'Ready to go about.' JC put the helm down, Baker hauled in the sheet, I felt sick and we started to run before the wind back to the point on the beach below Baker's little cabin. The world was a very 'uncomfy' place and I didn't like it at all – I wasn't quite past caring but not far from it. A line whistled past my head and I found myself hauling on it, then we grounded and the next wave carried us bit further up the beach. I was jolly glad the motion had stopped and it seemed to have become very peaceful all of a sudden and all I wanted was to curl up in the warm somewhere but JC grabbed me and said to Baker, 'We'll attend to this in the morning.'

'Aye, aye, sir three or four trips should do it.' My father walked me back to the hotel at a brisk pace telling me to hold myself upright.

'You'll like sailing once you are over this.' It was cold comfort and did not fill me with longing to try again, but by teatime I was better and by dinner almost fully recovered.

I woke to a bright and sunny morning with white fleecy clouds hurrying overhead and told myself the wind had dropped but the sea still looked just as rough. JC was in great form and as soon as we had finished breakfast we put on our oilskins and set off for Baker's cabin, where there was a dinghy on the slip with a cheerful looking youth standing beside it.

After saying 'Good morning', JC turned to the youth and said 'You know what to do', and then he turned to me 'I'm staying to talk with Baker. Now you get aboard and Tom will take you out.' I could not let him down but the sea looked very rough with the wind against the tide but I didn't learn till later that this always made a 'short sea'. Tom pulled from the shore and then at an angle to the run of the sea while I put scraps of cold fatty bacon on the hooks of a line. The dinghy pitched, it rolled, it sat on its stern, it wallowed and wriggled and I began to wish I had not eaten so much for breakfast.

After about ten to fifteen minutes, which seemed like hours, Tom said, 'I'm thinking you'm about ready to go ashore.' I was but he took his time pulling back to the beach where JC was waiting to grab me and make me walk.

He stepped out at a pace I never thought him capable of achieving and after about twenty minutes I was almost back to normal and did not demur when he said, 'Get aboard again and see how you do.'

Out into the waves again, pitching, rolling and wriggling, but after fifteen minutes of this torture, when I was sufficiently green, Tom thought I was ready to go ashore again. A brisk walk up and down the front for ten minutes or so and then back to the dinghy; pitch, roll, wallow, and wriggle again – the more the merrier. After twenty minutes or so I wanted 'terra firma' again but, after a brisk walk, keeping myself upright, the discomfort passed off. I returned to the dinghy thinking 'Oh, this is not too bad – I'd like to try rowing', so Tom and I changed places and I began to row – when I did not catch a crab. After half an hour, and getting really warm with my exertions, it was as though I had never felt seasickness – or was it? Was I cured? I pulled for the beach where JC was waiting, scrambled ashore, thanked Tom for his help and heard JC arranging for us to go out for a sail after lunch. JC walked me well past the hotel and some way beyond the lifeboat station before we returned to the hotel.

About half past two we put on our oilskins and went along to Baker's slipway where we found the yawl, *Jeannette*, all ready for us. JC and I got aboard followed by Baker who, after a brief look round, shouted: 'Let her go' and we rushed down the steep shingle into the waters of the Channel. I helped haul up the mainsail, then break out the jib, and haul in the sheets as we laid off on the starboard tack for the South Goodwin lightship.

I was sitting on the midship thwart when JC called me aft to take the tiller saying, 'Keep her going and keep her full on course for the South Goodwin.' He watched me for a short while and then went forward to talk with Baker.

'Bear away. You're too close!' Baker came aft to show me how to keep her on course, and after some further instructions they left me in peace but I was too busy to listen to their conversation.

Then I heard JC's voice above the noise of the wind and sea, 'We have been far enough. Give orders for going about.'

Uncertainly I said, 'Stand by to go about.' Neither of them took the slightest notice. I said it again, a bit louder. Baker smiled at me but JC resolutely took no notice. I shouted 'Stand by to go about' and paused to see if they had heard – they had and were watching me. I saw Baker lift the jib sheet and wink. I took a chance, 'Let go jib sheet, haul in main sheet.' Nothing happened; we sailed on. 'Ready about, let go jib, haul in main, now', as I put the helm down.

I rushed it a bit but we went about – 'jib in a bit – ease main sheet, hold it, belay.' Baker looked at JC and said with a smile, 'He'll do when he knows a bit more.' Then for the next half hour I was shewn how to go about, heave to, gybe and run before the wind and after a final heave-to I was given the tiller and told to set course for the pier. JC had told me a lot about ships but had never explained how a ship was sailed though his interest in the 'ships' I had on the moat at Capel House must have been far more informative than I was aware of at the time. I must have gained, unconsciously, a very useful grounding in the elementary precepts of sailing. That, and my father's way of assuming that I knew the rudiments of sail, gave me confidence and a determination to show him that his expectations were not ill-founded.

As we approached the beach Baker said, 'The relief boat is going out to the Gull on the day after tomorrow. Would you like to come?' JC was delighted at the proposal and I think would have gone even if there had been a full gale blowing.

In fact the day was fine and sunny with only a few white clouds and a light wind from the south. The big motor boat was already afloat by the staging and the relief crew were going aboard when we arrived with a large hamper of food and several crates of beer as well as practically the whole stock of magazines and papers from the nearby newsagents. These were all passed aboard and then half a dozen hands stretched out to help JC aboard. 'Thanks! I was a seaman once – I'll manage.' I felt a bit awestruck among these big hearty men but need not have had any fears. One of them said 'Go and sit by the helmsman. He'll let you take over when we are clear of the pier.' By this time JC was in deep conversation with the men and the initial shyness had quite disappeared – they were all chatting away recalling this and that incident but I was too busy steering to pay any attention.

So for about forty-five minutes I concentrated on steering for the wreck-buoy south of the Gull. As we neared the Goodwin Sands JC asked if we could be put ashore to walk a few hundred yards before boarding again. He told Baker that he had always wanted to walk 'on that piece of the earth that had wrecked so many vessels. Nearly had me on one trip in fog'. I steered for a shallow inlet which was pointed out to me as the helmsman throttled back the engine, and as I followed JC over the side someone said, 'Keep moving. Those sands are hungry and they will drag you down if you stand still. Walk north and you'll see a bit of a German submarine that went aground at the end of 1918.' JC and I splashed overboard and set off for our walk over the shifting sands. They seemed firm enough until you stood still when they came up over your shoes in an incredibly short time.

We walked round the fore end of the submarine but there was nothing that we could take as a souvenir. After about fifty yards we came to another inlet where the motor boat was waiting for us.

We scrambled aboard and continued our trip to the Gull where JC and I boarded by a rope-ladder and were met by the chief officer. Everyone seemed to know all about JC which surprised me, until Tom told me that he had sent a signal to his brother who was a member of the crew we were to relieve. There were other surprises in store for me as JC changed from the gouty invalid I knew, to an able and energetic seaman almost as soon as his feet touched the deck. It was incredible; he became positively nimble going up and down ladders, through hatches and wherever he went asking questions and making comments on the differences between this light-vessel and the ones he had seen out East. When he had been everywhere he was asked if he'd like to go aloft to the lantern. He turned to me, 'Watch the roll and do as I do.' The Gull, like any other light-vessel rolled in the lightest swell, the mast head cutting an arc across the sky of about 20 degrees each way. I watched my father step onto the rail and start to climb the ladder, pausing as she rolled towards him then going on again as she rolled away. I followed with Baker close behind me, did as JC had done and arrived in the lantern as Baker returned to the deck. JC went into all the technicalities with the officer, about cleaning the lenses, adjusting the light, and explaining to me how the mechanism worked which turned the lenses on their carriage. He congratulated the officer on the care and cleanliness which had obviously been expended on the light, then turned to tell me to follow him down. We arrived on deck and JC thanked them and asked them to accept the hamper and papers from us both. It was quite extraordinary: here was a man who had not been to sea for more than twenty years, frequently crippled in hands and feet by gout, scrambling about a rolling lightship as though it was his everyday occupation. He seemed to have lost nothing of the way of life at sea, balancing himself against the roll and looking years younger. After three cheers from the crew we re-embarked on the motor boat amid shouted invitations to come again soon and spend a couple of nights aboard as we set course for Deal. The sun was well round to the west by now and disappeared behind the houses of the town as we came alongside the staging.

We did not go sailing every day and when JC was busy I amused myself sometimes going for a trip in the motor boat with the holiday-makers or lending a hand on the boats and launching slips. Sometimes my mother wanted things from home when I would accompany Vinten in the Cadillac, or if my brother was with us he would drive over to Oswalds letting me drive on the quiet bits of the road.

One day we had gone over to Oswalds with my father and mother to see how the work was going and returned to the hotel a bit after midday when we saw that a sailing ship had dropped anchor about half a mile offshore to the south of the hotel. There was a north-easterly gale blowing and the sea was very rough, making it difficult to beat up Channel, so she was waiting for a change of wind and tide.

We went in to lunch and JC insisted on sitting in the place I usually occupied so that he could watch her during the meal. We had barely finished when he said 'Come on, let's put on our oilskins and sou'westers and go and have a look. Perhaps go aboard.' My mother was very perturbed but realised that my father had made up his mind so only observed that there was quite a sea running. JC replied, 'It's only a popple, wind against tide. Nothing to worry about.'

We set out for Baker's pitch, the wind and rain doing its best to stop us, and when we got near there did not appear to be anyone about, but JC had to satisfy himself and thumped on the door. The door opened and JC put his head in and shouted above the noise of the wind and sea to Baker, 'Can you take us out to that sailing ship?'

In a short while Baker appeared at the doorway: 'What? You want to go out to that Scandinavian vessel sheltering from the gale? You're not so young as you used to be you know, Capt'n.'

'Neither are you but if the lifeboat had to be launched you'd be the first man aboard. I want to be rescued from dry land.'

'Oh, all right then, come on men, get the motor boat out.' JC and I scrambled aboard followed by Baker and a couple of men while others put down the slipboards between the bows and the water's edge.

'Stand by to let go when Bob's ready with the engine.' Bob's head appeared from the engine casing and after a quick look round, he shouted 'Let her go.' We charged down the slope and floated off into the Channel. It was really rough but Bob had the engine going and we paid off to starboard, heading south for the sailing ship. We were lucky as the tide had just set southward so, although it was still rough, the seas were not breaking 'short' as we went about round the stern after passing down the portside and came up on the starboard, closing to within a few feet of the ladder hanging over the side just for'rd of the poop. We rose and fell with the waves, the helmsman holding level with the ladder as we moved slowly nearer her side. One minute we were looking down on her deck and the next looking up at her bilges and the barnacles on them.

JC said, 'Be careful how you come. Watch me.' He stood on the thwart with one foot on the gun'le waiting for the right moment to step across, landed on the rail and so down onto the deck in one smooth movement. I followed but not so neatly, nearly missing the ladder altogether, though I managed to arrive without too much water coming aboard with me to be greeted by the bearded Captain. He pumped our hands and smacked me on the back so hard, and at the wrong moment, that I careered across the deck and fetched up against a skylight.

My father explained who he was and after much talk the Captain turned to me and said, 'It iss goot, you too a captain vill be. It iss to learn yong you must, but yu'ff made a startment.' Presently one of the crew appeared carrying three heavy mugs and a black bottle to be hailed by the Captain with, 'Ah, it iss goot a drink you have.' This suggestion was not entirely approved of by JC who had very definite ideas as to what a schoolboy should drink even if he was shivering with teeth chattering in a bitter north-easter. However I had my tot of rum and felt better for it and while the Captain and JC talked I listened to the song of the wind in the rigging and felt the movement of the ship. JC was quite at home, enjoying every minute and so was I. Although it was the first time I had been on board a sailing ship, I found a sort of comfort in the noise of wind and water, a sort of rightness, which was indescribable. Maybe I had had a drop too much rum. We spent about half an hour aboard before JC reluctantly turned to me, 'Well. We must go. Be careful and watch me get across.' Then addressing the Captain he said, 'I am selfish enough to hope that I shall be able to come aboard again tomorrow morning.'

'Ach, maybe, but I must for Rotterdam use the wind and tide.' I watched JC make his return to the motor boat and then followed as it came close alongside. Then with shouted good wishes and waving of hands we drew away and headed for Baker's pitch.

When we came down to breakfast the next morning the wind had dropped to a strong breeze from the southwest. The sailing ship must have got under way an hour or so before because all that we could see of her was a spread of canvas away to the nor' nor' east as she cleared the north foreland. JC was most disappointed: it would not have taken much to persuade him to join the ship and make the passage to Rotterdam. After the meal we went along to Baker's pitch where JC was given a note and a small parcel which had been left by the captain. The note explained that the Captain could not miss the tide as he was due in Rotterdam but he hoped that he might meet JC again in the future and in the meantime would JC accept a box of cigars as a token of his visit aboard.

We sailed as often as we could and I was put at the helm of the little yawl while Baker and my father swapped yarns and recalled the years gone by. I was much too occupied to listen until one of them tried to catch me out by letting the jib sheet go or suddenly telling me to go about with a shout of 'man overboard' to rescue a cigarette tin which one of them had thrown. It was all good practice and, as I became more proficient, I enjoyed dealing with these minor 'emergencies' and having my mistakes corrected and the reasons explained for various courses of action. They were happy days but they passed all too quickly and, although I enjoyed going over to Deal in later years it was not the same.

There were times, I must confess, when JC seemed to expect too much of me or assume that I had far more experience than was the case. Later I realised that any harsh words were for my benefit and safety. He did not appear to have any anxiety for my safety at the time, though he must have felt anxious he did not show it, and in that way gave me confidence. Some three or four years after his death I took a party of small boys to Deal and was able to hire Baker's boat for a short trip. It was a bright sunny day with a calm sea so I was able to talk to Baker. He was very friendly and full of reminiscences of his service under my father and told me that JC's rather harsh way of treating young seamen was in fact the kindest method that could be devised. He said that there were many men who had served under my father who owed their lives and seafaring happiness to the way in which he had instructed them.

JC had a knack of asking people to do things rather than ordering them and I know, personally, that although his tone could be severe at times, one did what was asked willingly and without hesitation. This was all the more extraordinary when one takes into account that his command of spoken English was not perfect and quite often he used a word or phrase in an un-English manner. Yet I am sure that when he was at sea he was respected and liked for his qualities both as a man and as a seaman.

When JC made drawings for me at Capel House I knew they were good, though I was under ten years old, but just how good I only realised during our stay at Deal. He made a couple of sketches to illustrate the difference between a full-rigged ship and a barque. There was quite a row with the hotel because someone had tidied up the drawing while we were at lunch and it could not be found. JC was very annoyed about it as he never kept any sketches he had made to explain a point; when he was satisfied that I had understood he crumpled them up and burnt them. This burning of sketches at Capel occurred, or so I thought, because he did not want a lot of bits of paper lying about, but I have wondered since then whether the sketches brought back memories or recalled the disappointment at not being able to get a command.

It was not until we stayed at Deal that I really appreciated just how much he wanted to get back to sea. My mother told me during our stay that she was worried lest the call might be too strong to resist, but our stay came to an end, and our days of sailing in Baker's little yawl, *Jeanette*, became treasured memories.

14

Study – elm tree – drawing room – rented houses –
Leacon Hall – furnishing – Mrs Willard – Mrs C's
bedroom – JC's bedroom – the crew – Audrey Seal
– flowers – clothes – visit to the church – power of
observation – Milward

When one entered Oswalds by the front door my father's study was along a short passage to the right, while on the left was the door to the dining room. Straight ahead was an arch leading to the staircase-hall with the stairs on the left. Just through the arch was the door to the den and further on the door to the drawing room, both on the right.

The study was a pleasant room with a large semi-circular bow window, facing slightly north of east, which took up almost the whole end wall rising from a four inch high cill to within a few inches of the ceiling. Along the right-hand wall across a sealed-off window were bookshelves with deep cupboards beneath. On the left was the flank of the hall fireplace and on the back of this, facing the window, was a mock bookcase made up of a series of battens representing the edges of shelves between which were stuck the backs of old leather-bound volumes. It looked realistic but my father took an intense dislike to it, saying, 'It is like rows of skulls of old friends stuck to the wall. It must be covered with a decent curtain.' Facing the main bookcase was the fireplace with a simple marble surround to an old-fashioned basket grate.

In spite of the large window the room was not well lit as there was the stump of a large elm tree within about twenty-five feet but the tree was a source of pleasure to JC as it was the hunting ground for numerous tits, finches, tree creepers, sparrows and a pair of green woodpeckers. My father was very proud of them as they turned up each year but after a few weeks their tapping on the bark of the tree became very irritating and various noises were made until they departed to another part of the garden. We had a pair of kingfishers who frequented the banks of the stream but when this dried up they moved on to the lake in Bourne Park. JC was not an enthusiastic bird

South side of study at Oswalds

Oswalds, 1919–25. Lower bay window: Joseph Conrad's study; over front door:
his bedroom

watcher, he would only watch for a minute or so and he did not profess to know anything about them. I think that what interest he did show was on account of Richard Curle's curiosity and perhaps he hoped to stimulate my interest by asking their names, habits and diets. After dinner, at around eight o'clock, he would ask me to walk round the garden with him, strolling quietly along the paths watching out for owls of which there were several kinds in the vicinity.

On one occasion he got to hear that someone had shot an owl and he held a council of war with the gardeners and myself to find the culprit and put a stop to any similar activities. It was rather awkward as the culprit was the son of an old friend who was staying with us while studying farming, and whose idea of a farmer was someone who walked round with a shot gun blazing away at anything. However he was warned by my father asking me at dinner whether I or the gardeners 'had found out who the damned scallywag was who had been shooting owls'. Although I did not tell JC who the culprit was I am pretty sure he knew because the carrying around of a shot gun stopped from that day onwards.

The dining room was a long room which had been extended in the past by taking about three feet from the width of the hall. Two round timber columns had been inserted on the line of the original wall to support the wall above which separated my parents' bedrooms. On the left, the south side, were two windows and at the end was a fireplace with deep recesses either side. To the right at the end was a door leading to a service passage, a short cut to the kitchen. The windows were set in deep reveals which made the room rather dark and it was necessary to have the electric light on at meal-time except when there was bright sunshine.

The den, which I shared with my mother, was a dark room with only one window across which my mother's invalid chair was placed taking up the whole of the well-lit area. On the right as one entered the room was a large 'walk in' cupboard and on the left a large 'safe' door faced the window closing in the strong room. This part of the house was well built and I could play my gramophone and records without disturbing my father. My mother's chair could be folded up, and when pushed into the corner by the fireplace there was enough room for a quarter-size billiards table to be put up.

Further down the hall was the drawing room which when we first looked over the house had a full-size billiard table in it. A semi-

circular bow window matching that of the study took up most of the
end wall facing north-east and in addition there was a pair of French
doors leading to a paved terrace adjoining the loggia, all facing
north-west. This was the most poorly-lit room in the house, it was
loftier than any of the other rooms and the ceiling was divided into a
number of rectangles by deep beams. It was panelled for half its
height in 'public-house style' painted a faded grey white; the wall
above was covered with coarse sacking painted aluminium and this
with dark-oak parquet flooring made it even more like a cavern. It
was just an immense void with the strangest acoustics; a person
sitting in front of the fire could not hear people sitting on either
side!

During the years covered by these recollections people did not
seem to bother about redecorating either inside or out, I don't
remember the painters being in the house but then all the houses my
father lived in were rented. I have no memories of wallpaper books or
paint cards but this does not mean that my father was totally
insensitive to his surroundings, though he was able to ignore or
detach himself from his immediate environment. As far as I can
recall there were two exceptions, chocolate brown and Brunswick
green paint. He disliked the brown but hated the green. When we
returned from Deal we found that the repaired doors etc., had been
painted Brunswick green by the owner's workmen and to make
matters worse they had left an empty tin in the yard to confirm the
colour. JC was really angry and accused the owner of trying to insult
him and was all for going to see him about it, until my mother
pointed out that the owner knew nothing of JC's dislike of the colour.
My father accepted the fact, 'But my dear Jess, it is not only the
colour but the name of the damned mess. I won't have it – it's an
insult to decency!' Two days later all the offending doors had been
painted over with an 'honest' black, much more suitable.

Looking back it is obvious that the furnishing of Oswalds was
never given any serious consideration, my father had never given any
thought to it and just expected it to be ready to live in when he came
to take up residence after staying with friends during the move. My
mother did her best but her leg was giving her a lot of discomfort at
that time which made searching for suitable furniture almost impossible though she managed to furnish the study, den and dining room
and make four of the seven bedrooms on the first floor habitable.
Oswalds was much larger and had more rooms than Capel, a fact

Corner of drawing room at Oswalds

that was not fully appreciated due to spending six months in a large fully furnished house. Luckily for us we had a good friend in Mrs Grace Willard, an American lady, who came to my mother's aid and who undertook to find suitable furniture. The proposition must have been discussed by my parents but I think it most unlikely that they expressed a wish for any particular style of furniture, which was a pity, because neither of my parents liked the finished effect. To JC it looked 'like some damned stage setting', and to my mother it was too 'continental'. It had an ornate look with several pieces of French furniture, gilt chairs of Louis XIV period, much carved and painted settees and a lot of furniture of too delicate construction for every-day use to which JC took exception at having to warn guests to treat it gently.

The dining room was more sensibly furnished, albeit in a Victorian style, with good solid mahogany sideboard, chiffonier and table all having hideous mouldings and very very heavy. The chairs were an unfortunate choice, being made of beech, 'modern' and an unpleasant brown with 'rexine' seats, but the room stood up well to the every-day wear and tear of a family who were not furniture conscious.

By this time my mother had become 'Mrs C' to all of us. Her bedroom was over the dining room at the top of the stairs and had two windows overlooking the drive, a fireplace at the end with 'mirror glazed' doors to two deep cupboards either side. Between the windows was a very much carved and gilded console with a pink marble top and over it was an enormous gilt-framed mirror. Together they did duty as a dressing-table. Facing this was a double bed with Sheraton head and foot panels and a pair of night tables of similar design. To the left as one entered the room a large three-section mahogany wardrobe hid the door beyond which led into my father's bedroom.

Through a square opening was the door to my father's bedroom on the right and almost opposite was a passage leading to a flight of four stairs at the top of which was the wc and the bathroom. JC's bedroom always reminded me of the captain's cabin, definitely not a 'stateroom', with its austere lino on the floor, a plain mahogany chest of drawers to the left of the window, with a small mirror on it as a dressing-table. An iron bedstead with a 'diamond' spring and a hair-mattress, rather higher than usual, which was my father's wish. At the foot of the bed was an oak 'library' table covered with a red leather top with a pair of drawers, each end containing filing trays. There were several piles of books on it, W. W. Jacobs for light reading, de Maupassant, Flaubert, Galsworthy, Cunninghame Graham, various periodicals and a book, which has always been a mystery to me, *Out of the Hurly Burly* by Max Adler.

In the window stood an armchair of cherry wood, lacquered black, on which my father often sat to read for half an hour or so before 'turning in'. The fireplace was in the left-hand wall and beyond it was an opening leading into a clothes closet fitted with shelves and rails.

There was no proper central heating; only a few radiators in odd corners, too small to make any appreciable difference to the tempera-ture, and which helped only to increase the consumption of coal by the kitchen range. We had electric light from batteries charged by an immense paraffin oil engine driving a dynamo. Soon after we moved in it became obvious that the silencer was blocked with soot, but before it could be attended to the bolts holding the cover down broke, and the peace of the countryside was shattered by the thud of the exhaust. It was the chauffeur's job to look after the plant and keep it in order and initially he had quite a job, as the previous occupants had left everything in an incredible mess. It was more or less by accident that we discovered that the unevenness of the floor was caused by about four inches of oily rags and sawdust on top of the original concrete. Charles Vinten, the chauffeur, managed to dig it out and in the process found a whole collection of tools which had been preserved in the oily mess.

Our gardeners, Jack Burchett and Louis Ford, had quite enough to keep them busy throughout the year, as there were two kitchen gardens, each about a third of an acre, a Dutch garden with herbaceous borders, a bowling green and several hundred yards of box and yew hedging as well as a greenhouse and three fairly large cold frames. Most of the paths were of crushed brick with a few of laid bricks all of which had to be kept free of moss.

The indoor staff, the crew as JC called them, consisted of Arthur Foote, valet/butler, Edith and Florrie Vinten, housemaids, sisters of the chauffeur, and Mrs Sophie Piper who did the cooking under my mother's guidance, and if there were more than three guests for a meal extra help was enlisted from the village.

After her operation in Liverpool to make her leg stiff by dovetailing the bones together, my mother had to have a nurse and so Audrey Seal came to live with us. She was a cheerful and efficient person and soon became 'part of the family'. We were fortunate at Oswalds as all the staff, once they got over their initial nervousness, liked and respected my father who in turn took a very genuine interest in their well being and in that of their families. If anyone was ill or had suffered some misfortune he would find out all about it and, if he could help with either advice or finance, he did so. He would administer a mild ticking-off to anyone who 'didn't like to bother him' about something: a day off or having a friend to tea. He would say, 'Why didn't you ask? I won't eat you. I am not an ogre.'

It was not until we moved to Oswalds that my father showed the least interest in the garden and only then to call attention to an untidy path or hedge. However, he did like to see a well-kept flower bed though he never attempted any gardening himself, not even the removal of a weed. He never asked for any particular flowers to be grown, with one exception, mignonette, and he made a point of asking that it should be planted near the house where he could see it.

He liked to see well-arranged bowls of flowers but was disappointed if there was no scent. He would not have any flowers in his study or bedroom and did not like flowers on the dining table. If any of the creepers on the walls of Oswalds grew over the windows, or worse still if they tapped on the glass when there was a wind, orders went out to 'see that those damned things are cut down'. He liked having new potatoes, fresh vegetables, peaches and nectarines from the garden but as far as I know he never gathered them for himself. Occasionally he would pick a flower for a lady guest though he disliked wearing a button-hole, 'The damned thing will only die and besides what is the point of it, anyhow?' I remember Hugh Walpole coming in from the garden with a button-hole given to him by my mother and calling JC's attention to it. My father looked at him for a moment: 'Charming if you like to look like a vegetable!' Walpole seemed to go out of his way to try and create an atmosphere of jealousy or annoyance but JC had no time for anyone who tried to make a mischief.

My father could not abide untidiness in dress and ticked me off on many occasions before I got the message. It had to be a really hot day before he would let an undone shirt-collar pass without comment. When he was 'en deshabille' in dressing-gown and 'flannel bags' he still managed to look tidy yet he was in no way a fop. To take off one's jacket without first asking permission was the height of bad manners, and a reporter who did so was shown the door in double quick time, with the advice that he should learn how to behave before he came again. To ease one's tie and unbutton one's waistcoat was disrespectful and showed an untidy mind and a slovenly attitude to life. In hot weather JC did not put on a tie but had a loosely knotted scarf round his neck under a light dressing-gown but, if visitors called, Foote was told to show them into the drawing room while JC went upstairs to make himself presentable with a stiff collar and tie, waistcoat and jacket. He did not often wear a soft collar, which looked shabby, whereas the stiff high collar was more dignified and was worn by many of his friends, Hope, Pinker and Galsworthy to name but a few.

One afternoon I was sent from the lunch table to make myself presentable. I cleaned my clothes and brushed my hair and offered myself for JC's inspection. 'Yes, that will do, but remember another time. By the way I want you to come with me after tea.'

'Yes, certainly. Will we be going far or seeing anyone?'

'No, quite nearby.' After tea I fetched JC's hat and stick and waited for him by the front door.

'Come. It is not far.' We walked to the drive gate and turned right! I had expected that we'd go straight on to the forge but no, my father went through the churchyard gate and stopped to wait for me by the church door. I opened it and stood aside to let him pass in but he took my arm saying 'No. We go in together', then laid his hat and stick on the bench and entered and turned towards the altar. He stopped me with a slight pressure on my arm, bowed respectfully but did not make the Sign of the Cross. After a few moments we moved on, stopping to look at the memorials and stained glass, entered the sanctuary and went up to the altar, paused for a minute or so, bowed and took two paces backward before turning to retrace our steps to the door which we closed, quietly, behind us. Not a word was spoken while we were in the church. I was curious to know why he had not crossed himself, because my aunt, also a Roman Catholic, always did and I expected JC to do the same. As we continued our walk round the church I asked him why he had not done so.

'My boy, when you are aloft taking in canvas in a gale there is no one between you and death but the Good Lord and you cross yourself many times in the course of a voyage – I think He will pardon me – to make the sign now would be pointless – there is no need.'

We carried on, pausing now and then to look at some tombstone and then, as though thinking aloud he said, 'Profanity is the preserve of the devil'. Then as we passed through the lychgate he said, 'Don't assume that because I do not go to church that I do not believe, I do; all true seamen do in their hearts.'

My father never made any comment or remark on any aspect of religion to me, he never suggested that I should go to church and 'flew out' at my aunt for pestering me to go. 'Don't keep trying to persuade him – you will only drive him in the other direction. Besides he is young and has time to make up his mind as to the right decision in due course.' My aunt got no assistance from my mother in her endeavours but then Mrs C often said that she was an atheist!

There can be no doubt that my father had an extraordinarily retentive mind, a power of observation that was quite exceptional yet not deliberate in the sense that he never appeared to be making an effort to imprint a scene on his mind. Often he would ask me to describe a view which we had both looked at earlier in the day or on the preceding day and invariably he could add things to the view which I had seen but not appreciated, as he said I had only looked 'with half an eye'. Some evenings when I had a school-friend staying he would throw a handful of odds and ends on the table and say, 'You have thirty seconds to look at that lot before I cover it over while we each make a list of what is there.' We would look carefully and start making our lists after they had been covered. Sometimes there were twenty or more items of which my friend and I might get a dozen or so but JC would get all or nearly all of them. My friend protested that my father knew what the pieces were when he challenged us but even when we put thcm out he missed very few and nearly always won, though after considerable practice we could get fairly close to his total. The night before my friend was due to return home we had a grand session and on one occasion JC achieved thirty-six items out of a possible forty while we boys only managed around thirty. We often played 'observation' at school and I am convinced that it helped to improve my observation and memory.

While at Bishopsbourne my father met Frank Ashton-Gwatkin, son of the rector, who had a similar capacity for remembering things. When a meeting was held to decide on a suitable inscription for the memorial panel in the porch of the Conrad Hall in the village it was Frank Ashton-Gwatkin who suggested the text, giving the number of the page, and its position on the page and the edition of the book, as well as quoting the 'inscription' word for word. Although my father could 'get alongside' anyone, he was not able to do so on this occasion; it was one of the very few times when there was no rapport, and in spite of fairly frequent meetings their conversation was 'laboured' and awkward. I remember one evening after tea when JC called me to go with him to the forge for a chat with Milward, the blacksmith. On the way home he observed, 'You know these country people have more sense in their little finger than many of the intellec-tuals. They go straight to the point – their minds are not cluttered up with all sorts of opinions, most of which are barely understood. They are easy to talk to and learn from.' I commented that Milward could hardly be 'labelled' one of the country people. 'You know what I mean: a person who is self-taught, who has not had any academic instruction and who has used his own ability to learn and improve his knowledge.'

15

Quietness – sympathy – dress – Foote – breakfast –
shopping – Petit – Bing – Courts – Goulden – lunch
– afternoon runs – Ninnes – Romney Marsh – Deal
– dinner – cigarette jug

The first thing that would have struck an observer of our daily life
at Oswalds would have been its orderliness. We were not haphazard
or 'bohemian' and whilst we each enjoyed our own freedom we
were bound by an undefined 'time pattern' to a repetition of the
regularity of a life at sea. It was not the result of any specific instructions given by my father though he did like his meals to be 'on
time' with the exception of tea which was served any time between
four and five o'clock. Our lives – Mrs C's, JC's and mine – were very
closely interwoven and, to a certain extent, impinged on the lives of
the crew. There was respect between us and there was trust, a mildly
familiar but none the less definite caring for one another.

If anyone was ill it was a matter of concern for all of us and
enquiries would be made and help offered. Arthur Foote was always
at hand to help my mother, fetching her workbox down from the
bedroom in the morning and taking it up again at night. He seemed
to have a special sense if JC needed him. I would be talking to
him while he cleaned the silver when suddenly he'd put down the
cloth remove his apron and be half way to the study by the time
the bell rang. There was no question of it being a coincidence; it
happened too often, several times a week between meals, though
in the ordinary way JC would have given any instructions after
a meal.

The crew would be down by six thirty and the fires lit in the study,
dining room and Mrs C's bedroom. At eight o'clock morning-tea was
taken to those who wanted it, and at nine o'clock the gong was
sounded for breakfast. JC was seated at the head of the table usually
before anyone else and he expected me or any friends to be there on
time. It did not matter at what time he had gone to bed himself.

Quite often it was three or four o'clock in the morning, but he was always down to breakfast at nine o'clock sharp.

He did not have a great variety of dress for either summer or winter; a tweed jacket and grey flannel trousers, white shirt and stiff white collar though towards the end of his life he took to wearing shirts with soft collars of which he did not really approve, as they looked 'shabby' to him. Often in place of a jacket he would wear a dressing-gown over his shirt and trousers, a silk one in summer and a heavier one in winter, but if he intended going out or if someone was coming for lunch he wore a suit, always neat and tidy and in good taste.

Foote was always present at meal-times to see that my father had what he wanted; he would serve JC with whatever there was for breakfast from the hotplate on the sideboard, scrambled eggs, kidney and bacon, without too much fat, kippers or risotto warmed up if any had been left from the previous day. He was not a heavy eater and seldom had more than one or two pieces of toast with butter and honey or marmalade. He always had two cups of coffee, with three lumps of sugar, which had to be good, properly made in a jug, in the French fashion.

When he had finished he would ask Foote if anyone wanted to see him and if there was he would see them in the study or occasionally in the dining room. If the gardeners had any questions he sent a message to say he would come down the garden later on, or if it was raining he would see them in the loggia. If there were no instructions to be given, he would take me by the arm and lead me to the study and we would spend a quarter of an hour or so looking at the birds on and round the elm tree while I told him what they were and what they ate.

Most mornings he spent reading the papers until about half past ten, and then answered any letters that had come, then once or twice a week Vinten would be told to bring the car round to the front door where we would climb aboard and go to Canterbury. Most times we would go straight up the avenue of beech trees to the main Dover road and turn left along it, drop down through Bridge and so to the town, bearing left at the Gate Inn down the Old Dover road. At that time the New Dover road was a wide sandy track crossed at frequent intervals by diagonal water runnels between the Gate Inn and St Lawrence Road. We went straight down along Watling Street, on along Beer Cart Lane turned right into Stour Street and right again into Jewry Lane and so to the back yard of the Fleur-de-Lys Hotel where we parked the car. We would go through the hotel telling Mr Shepherd, the landlord, that we had left the car there and asking for any parcels that came to be put into it. My father nearly always made his first port of call at Mr Petit's, tobacconist, about eighty yards short of St George's Church, where he bought his supply of Caporal cigarettes. My father never quite lost the habit of taking off his hat when entering a shop. He always asked after the owner's health and family and was genuinely interested in their news, and never forgot to thank them for their enquiries about my mother's health. He spent quite a long time at Petit's shop, more as a friend than a customer; but then people had more time in those days to behave in a civilised fashion; money was not the only thing that mattered, respect, consideration and friendship counted for far more than they do today. Leaving Petit's he crossed the street to the chemists, Messrs Bing and Son; again the courteous approach and the precise information about his requirements to Mr Roots, the manager. At regular intervals he would ask for a large bottle of eau de Cologne for my mother which was obtained specially for us. From here he retraced his footsteps to the hotel with occasional deviations to Courts, the ironmongers in Butchery Lane, or to Mr Hamilton the wine merchant or to his brother the optician. It often happened that JC arrived at a shop when the owner or manager was attending to another customer. An assistant would be called to take over so that the owner could attend to my father, who appreciated the courtesy but always asked that they should carry on with what they were doing saying, 'I can wait.'

This brings to mind a day when I wanted to find my father after he had sent me on an errand. I had been into several shops and, at the last one, had been told that he had gone to Courts. As I approached the door of the shop a gipsy woman was coming out 'stern first' with a large basket of clothes-pegs and things on her arm. I stood aside to let her pass, but she paused and said: 'There's one of them furriners in there goin' all la di da. I don't trust 'en, d'you?'

Without stopping to think I replied, 'Yes, I do. He's my father.' A look of amazement spread over her face and then letting out a loud 'squawk' she bolted – maybe I looked fierce. Apparently she had been begging for old stock and Mr Court had got a bit short with her and told her to get out. JC had not listened to the conversation, saw her turn to leave and raised his hat – a subconscious reaction by him but completely misunderstood by the gipsy.

At least once a week he would turn into Goulden's, a large stationery and book shop, where Mr Gontran Goulden would be 'hove to in the offing' ready to meet JC as soon as he came into the shop. They would shake hands and then my father would be led into Mr Goulden's office where he would be shown any books that might be of interest or be asked to approve the galley sheets of some pamphlet that was being prepared for him.

Towards twelve thirty we would gather together in the private bar at the Fleur-de-Lys for a drink before embarking for the trip home. JC would have a whisky and soda and I would be given a ginger beer or a lemonade; the term 'soft drink' had not been invented and I shudder to think what JC's comments would have been about such an expression. We would get home just before one o'clock to be met by Foote who came out to open the car door, collect any parcels and then take JC's hat and coat. In cold weather my father used to wear a brown Havelock overcoat with capelike sleeves, it was so heavy that it was all I could do to carry it. I shall never forget Foote's look of amazement the first time he helped JC into it.

At one o'clock the gong sounded and we went in for lunch. If there were only the three of us the table would have been reduced to its shortest length. Mrs C always sat at the far end, nearest the fireplace, with her leg raised on a stool, while JC sat facing her and I sat at the side facing the windows. If we were alone my mother served the food and Foote took the plates and placed them before JC and me. The first course was soup, clear in summer, thick in winter and this was varied by spaghetti, ravioli, gnocchi, or macaroni. This was followed by a joint, chicken or fish or an omelette, but this last had to be cooked by my mother, otherwise JC would not eat it. However there were times when my mother was not feeling too well when she went into the kitchen and stood by Mrs Piper while she made it, and it was eaten without comment. Potatoes and the more ordinary vegetables were served English fashion with the main course, but sea-kale, young peas, asparagus and sliced beans, were served French fashion, by themselves. None of us took large helpings and by today's standards they would be considered small. My father did not like his plate to be overloaded and 'looking like the deck cargo of a tramp steamer'. He maintained that in order to enjoy food one should always have 'a little bit of stowage space left', which was far better

Gontran Goulden

than getting up from the table 'loaded to the gunnels'. For a sweet my
father was very fond of 'plum duff', suet pudding with raisins; other
favourites were apple tart and raspberries and cream. Milk puddings
of rice, tapioca or sago were not so popular nor was fresh fruit salad.
'By the time you have chopped up the fruit and added the brandy
you have no idea what you are eating, and you have wasted the
brandy!'

When the spirit moved us, Vinten would be told to bring the car to
the door and my mother would heave herself into the back with some
help, sit down on the near side and have her leg lifted onto a stool.

My father would go round and clamber in on the far side to sit beside Mrs C. Vinten would arrange the rug and adjust the rear screen then get into the driving seat. I sat beside him, also wrapped in a rug except in hot weather, and off we would go for a drive. Sometimes we went to Hythe to see Mr Ninnes at his antique shop, at other times we would go farther afield to Rye or Winchelsea. It took some years for Ninnes to accept me. This feeling was mutual because, when we lived at Capel, I was always a little nervous of him on account of his corpulence; I really thought that he might 'go pop' when I was a small boy. I was always intrigued by his special writing desk from the top of which a semi-circular piece had been removed to accommodate his 'corpulence'.

After leaving Ninnes we might go along the coast road to Dymchurch and on along the sea wall to St Mary's Bay where we turned onto a really atrocious track behind the sea wall. JC and I would descend and walk on the sands to Littlestone while Vinten took my mother along, very very slowly to the other end to wait for us. JC enjoyed these walks and would describe various incidents that had occurred along this bay, which I thought at the time, he made up for my amusement. In later years I realised that he had recounted actual happenings which he had heard from local people, like Mr Slingsby, Mr Post or our doctor of those days. Romney Marsh seemed to have an attraction for him and he never tired of being driven across it. At the end of our walk we'd get aboard again and go through New Romney, along the winding road through Brenzett, sometimes turning right here and going through Hamstreet and home via Ashford and Chilham, then along the downs to Bishopsbourne. Quite often these afternoon drives were broken by a visit to an inn for a drink, the more frequent ports of call being The Drum at Stanford and The Walnut Tree at Aldington on the supposed site of Shepway Cross where, legend has it, the captains of the Cinque Ports used to meet. The Saracen's Head in Ashford and the Fleur-de-Lys in Canterbury have both gone, demolished in the cause of 'progress'. JC was very abstemious and only had a single drink at a time. We used the lanes for our afternoon drives, which were more peaceful than the main roads though the surfaces were finished with crushed flints so that punctures were numerous. Living at the bottom of a valley as we did at Oswalds seemed to make my father more anxious than ever to get onto the 'lift' of a hill from which he could see the sea, the Thames estuary or the North Foreland. By turning right when leaving Oswalds and following the lane over the railway and along the valley to the left then right to Langham Park Farm there is a wide view of Pegwell bay and the Foreland which JC enjoyed. Another even wider view was from the top of the Downs behind Bridge on the road to White Hill and Street End.

I think my father's favourite seaside town was Deal, with Dover a close second. There was always a lot to see at Deal, barges with their brown sails, steamers, and quite often a sailing ship at which JC would gaze, oblivious to everything else, longing to be aboard. He would stay rooted to the spot until the ship disappeared, naming the sails she had set, but whether for my instruction or his own edification I could never decide.

Tea was usually around four thirty and taken in the den so as to save my mother from having to move, and consisted of bread and butter, jam and honey and cake. JC had a preference for seed-cake with butter and honey but rarely had more than one slice and always had a slice of lemon in his tea, which was China, and made rather stronger than was usual. If visitors called or friends were staying there were at least two kinds of sandwiches, and close friends were always given their preferences; Richard Curle liked salmon pâté or patum peperium, Don Roberto's choice was toasted sardine sandwiches while Edward Garnett liked cress and cucumber.

The period between tea and dinner was the 'social' time of the day when we discussed the happenings of the day or local news but never gossip if JC was with us – he did not approve! My father never stayed long if we had had tea in the den as it was too much like a rabbit hole. When friends were staying tea was served in the drawing room and my mother stayed to talk to them while JC cruised around ready to cart off to the study any guest if they became bored. He would cruise about in a similar manner if I took one of his close friends for a walk even if it was only round the garden, but he would never join us. I have wondered since why this was so. I don't think he thought that his presence would inhibit the conversation though I listened more than I talked when he was there, but that was how it ought to be; not that I was afraid to open my mouth but I lacked the experience to know when to speak. Around seven o'clock the gong would be sounded so that guests had time for a bath and change before dinner. Whisky and soda or a glass of wine was offered before the meal which was announced by another sounding of the gong at eight o'clock.

Dinner consisted of soup or an entrée, fish or chicken, followed by a sweet or cheese, except when friends were staying when there would be four or five courses with appropriate wines. Coffee was served at the table when we were alone, but in the drawing room when we had guests and as soon as one or two had had enough JC carted them off to the study – how he disliked that 'cavern' of a room. If a guest was musical, he or she would be asked to play the piano but this created problems on account of the weird acoustics of the room. One had to move away from the area immediately in front of the fire to hear the piano about ten feet away in the corner, and if anyone sang one could hear far better in the hall outside the room. I asked to come home from school when Paderewski came to stay, but the end of term examinations were considered more important. I heard later that he had played for my parents, and as it was a hot evening the windows were wide open and nearly everyone from the village came and stood on the lawn outside to listen. I was always surprised by the efficiency of the village 'bush' telegraph. Some people, of course, made it their business to know who was coming and when.

At about ten thirty a tray with a jug of tea, glasses in pewter holders, and a saucer of sliced lemon was taken to the study and for those who preferred it, a whisky and soda. The tea had to be in a distinctive jug so that it was not mistaken for another jug, which was full of water and into which my father put cigarette ends. Before we got a willow pattern jug for the cigarette ends and a plain cream-coloured jug with a lid for the tea several mix-ups had occurred. It was inevitable that a cigarette end should be put in the tea and for someone to try to pour a cup of tea from the cigarette jar. Luckily no harm was done.

No one went into the study between meal-times unless he or she was summoned, since it was assumed that JC was writing the greater part of the time, though not necessarily writing his books, because he often wrote letters, long ones to particular friends. In later years the afternoons and evenings were not often productive times for him, and it seemed to me that the night from ten thirty onwards, when the house was quiet, and when extraneous noises did not interfere, was the best time. Quite often he did not go to bed until three or four in the morning; he seemed to manage with very little sleep as he hardly ever dozed during the day and then only for ten minutes or so.

16

Anxious traveller – Burwash – games – billiards –
ping pong – no interest in cricket – colonels –
memory – cruising around – bezique – *The Rescue*

Although there were only a few times when I was with my father
whilst at sea I soon realised that he was much happier and more 'at
peace' with the world on board ship. On land he was an 'anxious'
traveller, fussing for a day or more before a long journey or for several
hours before setting off for a visit forty miles or so away. He disliked
being late for an appointment and always set out much sooner than
was necessary even allowing for the lack of reliability of the cars of
those days. He distrusted directions given by yokels and ancient
signposts and occasionally appeared to lose his sense of direction
even allowing for the bewildering twists and turns of the Kent and
Sussex lanes.

I remember a trip to Burwash to see Rudyard Kipling at his home,
Batemans. We stopped for lunch at the inn by the crossroads in
Hawkhurst as my father had been invited to tea at Batemans at four
o'clock. In spite of dawdling over our meal it was obvious that we
were going to arrive far too early. We left the hotel after two-thirty to
drive the seven miles to Burwash, JC in front by the chauffeur, Mrs
C, the nurse and I in the back. We crossed the valley and turned right
on the Moor, followed the road along and down over the Kent Ditch
and up to the main road where we turned left for Hurst Green. My
father had been fussing before we left the hotel, now he was display-
ing all the signs of annoyance, fidgeting and blowing through his lips,
'We'll be late, you'll see. Damn and blast.' Are you sure this is the
way? What did the last signpost have on it? If you see a native we'll
stop and ask the way.'

We had left the village and started to descend the long hill down to
Etchingham when JC spotted a roadman, knapping flints at the side
of the road at the first right-hand bend. 'Vinten, stop, stop, I'll ask

that fellow.' We pulled up near him but 'that fellow', wearing dark glasses to protect his eyes from the sparks went on with his job without looking up. JC leant out of the car and shouted 'Burwash?' 'That fellow' laid down his hammer, took off his glasses and gazed at JC, got up slowly and walked to the car and said, 'I know I be dirty, Guv'ner, but I'll wash when I gets home, thanks', turned his back and resumed his job without taking any further notice of us. JC was completely bewildered, shrugged his shoulders and waved to Vinten to drive on.

I have always marvelled at the way Vinten managed to keep a straight face, a completely wooden countenance, while we in the back dared not look at one another. Mrs C kept silent, realising that it was not the appropriate moment to try to explain the misunderstanding. In a couple of miles the nurse, Audrey Seal, and I were dropped off in Burwash with instructions to have some tea and be ready to return home soon after five. The visit must have been enjoyable as JC was in great form and very cheerful on the run home and roared with laughter when Mrs C explained the roadman's behaviour.

JC never took any serious interest in outdoor games and I do not remember his having played any ball games with me after we left Aldington. He would watch children playing with a ball and throw it back when it went wide but he never took an active part in any game . The only game in which he took more than a passing interest was billiards, but even that was not taken very seriously. We had a quarter-sized table in the den and JC would give me a game between tea and dinner occasionally but he really preferred the French type of table without pockets. He gave me a lot of advice on how to strike the ball when I first started to play and gradually my game improved until we were fairly evenly matched. When my brother was at home JC would watch us play, giving advice and encouragement with complete impartiality. If he was too busy to give me a game he would tell me to ask Foote to play provided that it did not interfere with his work.

I had a large playroom next to my bedroom at the west end of the house where I had a full-size ping pong table. Often on wet afternoons Foote and I would have terrific tussles which JC would come to watch. Several times he tried to play but his gouty hands and wrists were too stiff to allow rapid movements though when he did manage to return the ball it was always well placed. He was not interested in any outdoor games and on the rare occasions when my brother had friends in to play tennis he did not watch. He gave donations to the local cricket club and to the flower show but took no further interest in them; he'd ask Burchet, the gardener, if he had won anything at the flower show and congratulate him if he had been successful. He invariably bought tickets for all the local entertainments which he would give away and I do not remember him ever attending in person.

Two retired colonels who lived nearby tried to persuade my father to go to Canterbury cricket week with them. Their lives were devoted to watching cricket and they went to all the matches they could. They arrived one afternoon in time for tea and very soon monopolised the conversation, relating their reminiscences of various matches they had watched until JC got fed up. 'I am totally unable to comprehend why a man hitting a ball with a piece of wood can produce a state of near lunacy in people who one would assume were otherwise apparently sane.' They had the grace to apologise but that tea-party came to an abrupt end.

Later on one of them invited my parents to tea and when my father and mother arrived on the due day they were met by the butler who apologised for his master's absence, but he was unavoidably detained! Would my parents please arrange to come another day? The butler, a great admirer of JC's books, went on to say, 'If you will forgive me, sir, I would suggest that you come when the cricket season has finished.' As it turned out my father never did enter this house as both the subsequent invitations were forgotten by the colonel.

The other colonel invited JC to his house to play chess, but after some three or four visits my father declined to go again as his opponent was so slow that my father lost patience with him. The result of this was that JC decided to take me in hand and improve my game, so two or three times a week after dinner we got out the chessmen and board and spent a couple of hours playing through the games in Capablanca's book. We played every game in the book, JC reading the moves, stopping where Capablanca had made a comment, so that we could write down our own observations. At the end we would compare notes and argue over various alternative moves. My father's comments were very similar to those in the book but sometimes there were wide divergencies of viewpoint and we would play the variations through, making notes of our reasons for our moves. After a time we would play the first six or seven moves from the book and then play on. Then later on 'straight' games without reference to the book, JC handicapping himself by surrendering a rook, a knight and three pawns. Gradually over the weeks of the holidays I managed to play well enough for his handicap to be progressively reduced until we played 'level'; and then after a series of drawn games came my first win. I don't know which of us was more pleased – I think JC was. He had tried to beat me and I had tried as hard – JC was not one to let his opponent win, though he played the game for the game's sake and he didn't have to win to enjoy the game.

Sometimes he would start writing immediately after dinner, a favourite time for him when the noises of the daylight hours had ceased and the shadows could be 'peopled' with his characters. He wrote in a small pool of light from a single reading-lamp with a dark shade, and when it was time for me to say goodnight I would enter quietly, place a hand on his shoulder, give him a filial kiss, and retire as quietly as I had come. He would look up, smile and return to his writing. This would be about half past ten and I then went upstairs, kissed my mother goodnight and went along the passage to my room, got into bed and read for half an hour or so before switching off the light.

Sometimes, not very often, I would hear my father's footsteps coming along the passage and up the three stairs to my room just as I was dozing off. He'd knock on the door and come in, 'Ah, you're still awake then. Come down and give me a game of chess.' At other times it might be between midnight and one o'clock when I would feel his hand on my shoulder and hear him ask me to come down for a game. I would put on my dressing-gown and slippers, brush my hair and descend to the study to find the chessboard set out and a glass of lemon tea waiting for me. Sometimes, after playing a few moves he would get up and walk over to his desk, sit down and start writing. I would wait, listening to the little scratching noises of the pen on paper, until I dozed off. At other times we might make twenty moves before he got up to go over to his desk and I would sit studying the board before starting to nod only to be wakened by a hand on my shoulder. 'It's time to turn in. It is your watch below.' And I would retire to bed.

Next morning at breakfast he would look at me and say, 'That last move of yours was a mistake. I have only to move my queen to king's bishop three and you will be checkmate in two moves.' It was a bit disconcerting when your opponent remembered the position of the pieces and the last move, when you believed he was thinking of something else.

People have said when I have told them of this recollection that my father was being rather selfish in getting me out of bed, but it never struck me in this way. I was flattered that he should ask me to get up and play chess with him in the 'small hours'. There was no compulsion about it but there was a special kind of novelty in sharing the shadows surrounding the pool of light on the chess board, a silent communion punctuated by the occasional click as a move was made or a 'check' called. I realised fairly soon that the mental effort of playing chess helped my father to realign his thoughts so as to overcome an 'impasse' for the arrangement of words or the construction of a phrase to convey some subtle meaning.

I remember one game which we had started late at night and over which I had fallen asleep after he had left the board. The game had been left on the board in the cupboard in the den for a couple of days when he said, 'You had better put the men away. We'll finish that game some other time.' I made a plan of the board and carefully marked in the positions of the pieces, put it in the box with the chessmen and put it away in the cupboard. About ten days later after dinner he said, 'Come, we will finish that game of chess. It was my move.' I agreed and went to fetch the board and the men from the den and took them to the study. 'Can't you remember where the pieces were?' my father asked as I unfolded my plan. 'What on earth do you want that for? You ought to remember their positions. Here, give me the box and I'll put them out.' Without looking at my plan he put each piece in its right position without any hesitation. This would have been an achievement for anyone after one night but quite ten days had elapsed, and I am quite sure he had not looked at the board after he had got up and started to write nor had he seen my plan for long enough to memorise it. He did not ask me where I had put the chess set though I had not put it in its usual place in the study. When he left the board to start writing he must have been thinking about what he was going to write and not about the position of the chessmen.

I have no doubt that he had a photographic (for want of a better word) mind of quite an extraordinary capacity for the retention of 'images' of every-day things. In order to improve my ability to remember things he would spend an evening with me trying to solve the chess problems in the newspaper. We would each have a piece of paper on which we wrote down the moves and the reasoning behind such moves and then we would compare our notes. It was not until we had completed our notes that we would play the moves on the chessboard. JC usually found the answer long before I did though there were the odd times when we tied, which always gave him the greatest pleasure.

Some evenings he'd play bezique with my mother who certainly preferred to win and would crow over my father implying, so it seemed to me, that it was her greater skill with cards that enabled her to win. However JC didn't take it to heart though he did like the game to be a close run thing with scores nearly equal.

If my father saw my mother, brother or myself reading a book he would cruise around and pounce on it if we put it down while we went out of the room. When we returned the book had vanished and could not be found; most mysterious until we realised what was happening. A day or so later the book reappeared in exactly the same place from which it had vanished, and open at exactly the same page. My brother and I got a bit fed up with losing our books so we decided to have a 'dummy' reading book, usually a dissertation on some really boring subject. If JC was 'on the cruise' we hid the book we wanted to read and substituted the dummy which we put down when we left the room, sometimes at JC's behest to fetch something. The book would disappear and then after an hour or so JC would search out one of us and ask us not to leave our books lying about! Nothing more was said though I am pretty sure JC knew what was happening and eventually he did let us finish our books before carrying them off. He never recommended books to me or suggested that I should read certain books, except Marryat and Jacobs. If he saw me take a book from the shelf he would ask me what it was but he never suggested that I should read any of his books nor did he ever discuss them with me. His literary life was very much his private preserve as far as the family was concerned. He did occasionally talk to my mother about his work but if I came into the room the subject was dropped as though it was some scandal.

The Rescue was the first book written by my father that I read and when I had finished it I asked him to sign it for me which he did 'To John with his father's love, 1920'. He handed it back to me, 'Now get out.' I left the room closing the door quietly and as I walked away I heard him blow his nose with terrific violence. At no time did he like to show emotion but on this occasion I believe he came very close to it. After lunch he called me into the study and said, 'I always give your mother one of the first copies of a new book. Of course I sign it and later on she will give them to you so that you will have a set of my books.' After a pause: 'That's all.' A few years after his death I learnt that the books had been acquired by an American collector and so I have only one book of my father's stories inscribed to me personally.

I suppose that I should blame myself to some extent for this state of affairs but it never occurred to me that my father's wishes would be ignored and that so few personal things of JC's should be retained. My mother was, relatively, well provided for but she never discussed with me the sale of any object; in fact it was all done without my knowledge so I was presented with a *fait accompli* about which nothing could be done.

17

Mrs C short of occupation – telegrams – burst tube
– Christmas lunch – Corsica – books –
Cunninghame Graham – Galsworthy – broken belt
– ability to switch thoughts – Walpole – carpenter –
ticking-off for poor Latin

My mother found the peaceful routine at Oswalds rather boring though JC and I enjoyed it. Now that JC had a secretary, Miss Hallowes, my mother had time on her hands with no typing to do, and with Mrs Piper doing practically all the cooking she had no cause to stand over a hot stove. Audrey Seal took breakfast up to her in bed and Sophie Piper went up to fetch the tray and receive instructions for the day, then my mother would get dressed and come downstairs about eleven thirty or midday. Sometimes she went to the den and sat on her special chair until lunchtime, sipping a whisky and soda brought to her by Sophie, at other times she went to the kitchen if there was any need for her to supervise some dish.

I thought on a number of occasions that having so many people to wait on her did not really suit her, she was happier in spite of her damaged leg, to be up and doing something. She filled her time with writing letters, knitting and crochet work and when these palled she read novels, good, bad and indifferent. Very occasionally Audrey Seal would be asked to play bezique or dominoes. Mrs C liked being driven about the countryside and once a fortnight was taken over to see her mother, Mrs George, living near Cranbrook, but she was never interested in any of the places she visited and if we stopped in a village I was expected to find something to buy for her.

Friends often came to stay and she looked forward to their visits though most of them came to see my father, and only spent a relatively short time with Mrs C though there were exceptions. Hugh Walpole always spent an afternoon and evening with her, likewise Mrs Dummett and Mrs Hope. Sophie Piper provided the local news and a certain amount of gossip of which JC did not approve.

Mrs Conrad and John at Oswalds, 1922

There was no telephone at Oswalds, the nearest public box was at Bridge Post Office, about a mile and a half away through Bourne Park. Telegrams were brought from there by a telegraph boy but we had to provide our own boy when we wanted to send a message. When I was at home JC would send me to Bridge to send off a 'wire' or he would ask Louis Ford to take a message when he went home in the evening as he lived in Bridge.

Between the drive to the front of the house, and the garage yard was a plantation of box bushes, seven or eight feet high, through which a narrow cùrved path had been cut which saved the long walk round the two drives. I always used this path and one morning when I had to deliver a message from JC to the chauffeur I went that way. As I walked through I heard the car engine running, making an unusual noise and as I emerged I saw that the bonnet was open and a hosepipe was attached to the engine-driven tyre pump which was connected to the inner tube of one of the tyres. Vinten had obviously left the engine running while he went to fetch something and I was just going to walk past the car when I caught sight of an immense shiny black object which I realised was the very much over-inflated inner tube. I went to the opposite side of the car and switched off the engine and then, keeping as far as possible from the monstrous tube, I went in search of Vinten. He was in the electric-light plant room and came out in response to my shouts and followed me back to the car. He took one quick look and pulled me behind the door as the tube burst with a shattering din, the heat of the sun had proved too much for the rubber. The noise deafened us so we did not hear JC come into the yard while we collected the pieces of rubber.

'And what, may I ask, do you think you are doing making that damned row?'

'I was blowing up the tube to find a puncture, sir, and forgot about it.'

'Well, it would seem that finding the puncture is no longer of importance but next time stay by it and see that it doesn't happen again.' Then, turning on his heel, JC went back into the house. When Vinten went to be paid he used to take a written note of the money he had spent during the week on petrol, oil, tyres etc. When he went in with his list the next week he had not included the cost of the new tube and JC wanted to know why.

'Where is the amount for the tube? Don't tell me you repaired it. How much was the new one?' Vinten mumbled something, only to be told to speak up.

'I ruined it, sir, though it had been repaired several times.'

'Quite, quite, so it was not new?'

'No sir.'

'Then how much was the new one?' A figure was mentioned.

'Very well, I'll pay half, but don't go making a habit of blowing them to bits. You'll frighten our neighbours and we'll get a bad name in the village.'

The summer holidays came to an end and I returned to school. Letters from home reflected a fairly peaceful atmosphere, though my mother's knee was giving trouble and there was talk of another operation being necessary. Then a month or so later I got a letter saying that her leg was better following a minor incision which had been made to drain away some fluid, and on the strength of this my parents were going to motor down to Corsica at the end of January and would be away for about three months.

The term ended about a week before Christmas and I returned home to find a certain excitement in the atmosphere in anticipation of the trip across France to Marseilles en route for Ajaccio. Vinten was preparing the car and applications had been made for his passport and that of Audrey Seal, my mother's nurse, who was going with them to look after Mrs C. They were to leave a couple of days after I returned to school. What with the general excitement that a trip abroad created in those days and JC's anxiety when preparing to set out on a journey the days sped by with bewildering rapidity. It was just as well that we never altered our day-to-day existence for the Christmas holiday. There were no shopping expeditions, no decorating the house with holly, though a bunch of mistletoe was hung in the hall and ignored. Neither my mother or JC ever referred to the traditional Christmas decorations, and I was unaware of them for many years.

On Christmas Day lunch was at the usual time of one o'clock and consisted of roast turkey, vegetables, Christmas pudding with a brandy sauce, mince pies, a few crystallised fruits, dates and figs. We had our usual drinks, cider, whisky and soda, and water for me, followed by coffee, and a box or two of crackers. On Boxing Day we had cold turkey and salad, warmed-up pudding and pies and, if any had been left, the last of the crystallised fruits. By the end of the day all the festivities were over and we returned to our normal routine. I was always given a present and, in return, gave some little thing to each of my parents; the crew had something extra added to their wages. All the delivery boys and anyone who brought things regularly to the house received a present of money and my mother always made up parcels for any members of the crew who had families.

Carol-singers were listened to and given a donation but not until they had been through most of their repertoire. No member of the family went to church though some of the crew went to the early service. In retrospect it seems that the aim was not to let anything interrupt our existence. Christmas and New Year came and went with hardly a ripple on the surface of our lives, and so it was until my wife and I set up a home of our own.

A short while after Christmas I was in my room which overlooked the yard by the engine room, building a model car that JC had ordered, which was to be complete with 'proper steering, gearbox and differential and driven by the electric motor you were given at Christmas'. I was making up the chassis and vaguely aware of the regular thumping of the exhaust of the engine on the other side of the yard. Suddenly there was a crack like a stock whip and the engine raced and then slowed down as the governor took over then speeded up again and slowed down. I rushed down the stairs to tell Vinten that something was wrong and we ran into one another at the corner by the garage; after disentangling ourselves we headed for the engine room where he slammed over the 'half compression' lever while I turned off the paraffin to stop the engine. He picked up the driving belt which had broken along the line of the clasps of the connector and had just observed that the belt was a bit long so could be re-used, when JC appeared in the doorway.

'Now then what's the matter – can't you look after the engine properly?'

'Well, sir, the belt broke and—.'

'Any damned fool would know it broke. It ought not to have broken. You can't have been attentive. Never looked to see if it was all right before starting up eh?' He glared at Vinten and then went indoors.

It always struck me as uncanny how JC invariably went straight to the centre of any trouble, especially on this occasion which must have broken his concentration because I had been in to ask him a question a bit earlier about the car I was building, and had been told to 'Get out'. He was deep in thought on some composition and I knew from previous experience that his concentration would be intense until lunchtime.

On these occasions I had the impression that he was preoccupied and I often wondered whether he had to come back from the world of the story he had created, or whether he could switch off those

thoughts in order to deal with the immediate present. I never
screwed up sufficient courage to ask him because he always kept his
literary life very much to himself and at no time that I can recall did
he make any remark which could be interpreted as referring to his
writing. There were very few friends with whom he discussed his
work; that is, the actual construction of a plot or the creation of an
atmosphere against which to set a story. I think it would be right to
name them in the following order: Marwood, Cunninghame
Graham, Curle, and perhaps Garnett, though he always struck me
more as an observer than adviser. Graham's knowledge of South
America no doubt helped to fill in some details of Costaguana (the
setting for *Nostromo*) and Curle's knowledge of the Far East was also
appreciated by JC. On those rare occasions when I followed JC and
Richard Curle into the study after dinner, I sat near the door so that I
could leave the room without disturbing their conversation. I did not
enter into the conversation and they soon forgot I was there, and the
shadows outside the circle of light became peopled with hazy figures,
sometimes with faces and shapes, but often without features when
they spoke of people they had both known. I felt I was eaves-
dropping at times but I was sitting in their full view though the
feeling was so strong that I would creep away in half an hour or so.
My father did not encourage me to join him when Don Roberto was
with us and anyhow I would not have understood much of what they
were saying as it was mostly French with some Spanish. When
Walpole was staying I didn't want to listen to their conversation
which frequently sounded acrimonious, and I was aware of the
provocative remarks made with object of 'creating a situation' which
JC was careful to ignore or treat as a joke.

At lunchtime on the day the belt broke JC asked me what Vinten
had done about it and I explained that it had been long enough to be
rejoined and used again by moving the dynamo along its adjusting
rails.

'That's good. By the way, did you retrieve the spanner that Scally
was walking off with?'

'Yes, I put it on the bench.'

Scallywag, or Hadji-the-second, was the son of Hadji the dog we
had at Capel House, a clever mongrel 'collie' who was very easy to
teach, but his one failing was that he did not know when to stop and
he had to be watched if there were any tools lying about, as he would
cart them off and bury them. I used to get him to carry in the basket

of vegetables to the kitchen from the garden, and he would sit for several minutes with an unlit cigarette in his mouth if he thought he was being photographed.

One day I was cycling round the garden in the morning when a carpenter arrived to repair the greenhouse. I had stopped at the top of the path leading down to it and saw the man put down his bag of tools and disappear round the corner. The next moment Scally came through the door beside the greenhouse from the bowling green, sniffed the bag, picked it up in his mouth and trotted off along the path by the stream towards the house. I went to see where he was taking it and saw him drop it when someone shouted at him so rode on into the bowling green, and as I dismounted I caught sight of JC coming down the path I had come along. He was looking for Louis Ford, the gardener, because he wanted a telegram sent off when he went home for lunch. JC looked in the greenhouse and as he came out was confronted by a mystified and rather cross carpenter looking for his tools. They had not met before and the man asked, in a very surly manner, where his tools were.

'My good man, I am not the keeper of your tools and I do not know whether you brought them. When you ask a question to which you want an answer show some respect for the person to whom you speak.'

'I'm not your good man. I put the tools down here and they're gone, and don't you try to—'. Ford appeared, with the bag of tools, coming along the path by the stream.

'What's the idea Fred, leaving your tools down by the bridge?'

'I'm sure I never—.'

'Well that's where they were, so now you've got them you can get on with the job.'

'No, I've 'ad a look an' I'll 'ave to get some wood an' stuff from the yard and I'll take me tools with me afore they get lost again.' Ford told my father that the carpenter was 'a bit of a funny one' and he would probably be back in a day or so. Then after arranging for Ford to take the telegram JC returned to the house. At lunch he described his encounter with the carpenter and was quite amused by the whole affair. I didn't say anything about the dog having taken the tools, it never occurred to me to do so.

Some days later I was overhauling my bicycle before sending it back to school. I had blown up the front tyre, laid the pump on the ground while making an adjustment, then turned my attention to the back wheel, groping for the pump as I did so. It was not there and although I searched everywhere it could not be found. I asked the chauffeur if he had seen it or if anyone who might have borrowed it had been to the house. We looked at the dog but he was apparently fast asleep in the sun and I had not seen him move. I told JC of my loss but apart from giving me some money to buy another pump he was not interested, and several days later I returned to school.

The term started badly for me by getting hauled over the coals about my Latin, a subject which I found tedious and rather pointless.

'How do you think your father could write such good English if he had not studied Latin?' my form master asked me.

'Please, sir, he learnt his English before the mast on the collier brigs out of Lowestoft and from the local papers.'

'Oh, come! That is a tall story. I shall write to your father about your Latin.'

'Yes, sir.'

There seemed no point in protesting or repeating my assertion or pointing out that any Latin he may have learnt would have been while he was in Poland. About a week later, after the Latin lesson, I was told to wait behind when the rest of the boys went out. I was not much worried, my preparation had not been quite so bad as the previous week and I felt no trepidation when I was called up to the master's desk.

'I owe you an apology for not believing you when you said your father learnt his English before the mast.' He paused, then handed me the letter he had received from my father.

'Perhaps you would like to read his letter?' I read it and then went back to the beginning of the last paragraph 'I am surprised that you, along with so many other Englishmen, make the mistake of writing "different to" instead of "different from".'

I smiled as I thanked him for letting me read it. He said: 'We are not all perfect and we can all learn even when we have left school. I shall have this framed and hang it in my study.'

Who changed? I or the master, my attitude or his? What made us change? JC's letter perhaps, but the fact remains that my Latin improved and my respect for the master increased and he was genuinely happy that I soon became one of the top four in the class.

My mother wrote regularly telling me all the news from home;

there were fairly frequent reference to tools being lost and vague remarks about something being done about it. Then came a letter to say that the car would be calling for me a few days before the official end of term to go with JC to Leigh, near Reigate, where J. B. Pinker lived.

18

Picked up at school – Leigh – coach and four –
Goudhurst – room in the roof – scars of a duel –
Saturday cricket – coach trip to Deal – JC pilot –
Thursday cricket – Milward – manners – maid

Soon after noon on Monday, 25 July the car arrived and JC went to
have a word with my housemaster while I took my luggage out to the
car. Presently he reappeared and we went down to the hotel in the
town for lunch before proceeding on our journey to Leigh. JC said
nothing as to the reason for our visit and I didn't question him as I
liked staying at Bury Court where we arrived at teatime.

After tea JB, as Mr Pinker was called by all of us, asked my father if
he'd 'like to have a look?' I went along with them, JB in a state of
suppressed excitement and JC smiling at his efforts to control it. We
went into the stable yard and there in all its glory stood an old
fashioned coach glistening in the afternoon sun as two men continued to try to make it shine even more. It really was as JC remarked
'magnifique et incroyable'. It had obviously been well cared for
because the upholstery was practically unmarked and everything
about it was in first-class order. JB suggested that I should give a
hand getting it ready – I was not too keen but being a guest I agreed.
He looked at my father and said, 'Have you said anything?'

'No.'

Then he explained: 'Tomorrow we shall leave here on the coach
for Goudhurst where we shall spend the night and then on the next
day go on to Oswalds. I tried not to show my doubts and more or less
succeeded.

Morning came and I could hear the noise of horses' hooves and
other noises 'indicative of travel' as JC said when he came to see if I
was getting up. He brought a small suitcase with him which we were
to share for the overnight stop at Goudhurst. I put my things in it and
took it along to where the cases of the Pinker family had been
collected in the hall. A little before ten o'clock the coach with four

J. B. Pinker's coach and four leaving Bury Court, Leigh, near Reigate, 1921. From left to right: coachman, Ralph Pinker, John Conrad (white shape behind J. B. Pinker's right arm), J. B. Pinker, Mrs Pinker (between her husband and Joseph Conrad), Joseph Conrad

horses was brought round to the door and the cases were loaded into the 'boot', a compartment under the rear seat right at the back where the coachman and stable lad would ride. The rest of the cases were loaded into the Cadillac which then rolled away on its journey to Oswalds.

JB took his seat on the box, resplendent in grey frock-coat and top hat, a new waterproof rug draped closely over his knees with JC sitting beside him, likewise wrapped in a rug. I could not help thinking how unnecessary they were as the day was bright and sunny and soon would be quite hot. Behind, on the next seat, I sat between Mrs Pinker and their youngest son while the rest of the party sat inside the coach. JB gathered up the reins, took the whip from its holder and nodded to the men holding the horses' heads, which they released. Then as the coach moved past they swung themselves onto the boot. With the coach-horn sounding we turned out of the drive towards the village, left for Charlwood, right then left again for Lowfield Heath and Rickman's Green. About a mile further on we took a sharp left turn at Copthorne Common, then on to Felbridge where we joined the main road through East Grinstead and so on to Forest Row where we stopped at the inn for lunch.

The weather was fine and warm and the sedate pace gave us plenty of time to see the countryside as it rotated slowly about us. After lunch we re-embarked and rolled on through Hartfield and Withyham, Groombridge and Tunbridge Wells where we kept left along the top of the hill and round onto the Pembury Road, then left just before Lamberhurst for Goudhurst. We descended the long gentle hill down to the railway crossing by the River Teise and started up the long steep hill rising some three hundred feet to Goudhurst village. About half way up we stopped to rest the horses and then continued up the last steep bit, turned right and then left into the yard of the Star and Eagle Hotel just below the church.

We clambered down and after going to our rooms for a wash and tidy up we went down for a late tea. There had been very little traffic and what there was behaved well and showed consideration for the coach and horses, which had raised quite a lot of dust on the crushed flints of the road surface. We exchanged opinions on the trip so far and everyone commented on the amount of detail in the countryside that the leisurely rate of travel enabled them to see. My father and I were not wildly enthusiastic but we enjoyed the experience and JC displayed his usual flair for observation, calling my attention to the more unusual objects we passed. Later, when he and I were getting ready for dinner, he observed that the 'famille Pinker' seemed to travel with their eyes closed as they had exclaimed at some of the things JC and I had mentioned that we had seen on our journey.

JC and I shared a room 'in the roof' over the lounge and part of the dining room, a rather long and narrow room with the ceiling sloping in on either side from a height of about four feet. The door was in the middle of one long side with a dormer window opposite and the two beds were alongside the end walls with a night table and lamp to each. We dined fairly early and we were all feeling sleepy after a day in the fresh air but JC sat talking with JB afterwards and I went up to bed and was fast asleep by the time he came up.

I was woken in the morning by the houseman bringing in two cans of hot water and our cleaned shoes. JC was leaning on the window board looking out over the South Downs where patches of mist softened the outlines of the hills and a haze gave promise of another fine day. He had his pyjama jacket in his hand and as I got out of bed he said:

'How very like some parts of Poland it is. I had not realised there were so many pine trees on these slopes.'

I was not interested in the view, however much like Poland it was. I was looking at some scars just below his left shoulder in the pectoral muscle, the white weals looked as though they had been made with a sword or cutlass. There were two about an inch long, tapering together towards the top and another pair about the same length forming a cross slightly below and to the left of the first pair. They appeared to be quite clean, straight cuts but I could not see whether there were any marks of stitches. He looked at me as though to read my thoughts and slowly I got over my surprise and looked him in the face as I realised that he was talking to me.

'Later on you will learn to fence but I doubt if you will ever fight a duel, though it is as well to be prepared. You never know what jealousy may lead a man to do. He was jealous of a friendship extended to me in Marseilles – we fought a duel and he wounded me sufficiently to satisfy his honour.' Ideas had raced through my mind: were they wounds received from a fight with cutlasses, repulsing a boarding party perhaps? I was a bit lost when I heard that those wounds had been the result of a duel. We finished dressing in silence and JC returned to gaze out of the window while I put our things in the case and as I snapped the catches to, he said,

'Leave it there. The man will bring it down presently.' Then linking his arm in mine, we went down to breakfast. No further reference was ever made by my father to the Marseilles episode and I never tried to pry into what was for him a very private matter.

Breakfast over we prepared to journey on and after much activity, 'whoas, git backs and stands' we were ready to move off a few minutes after ten o'clock. We drew out of the hotel yard to the sound of the coach-horn, turned right up the hill between the crowds on either side and, skirting round the churchyard, rolled along at a brisk trot through Sissinghurst and Biddenden. There seemed to be an awful lot of people lining the road to watch us go by. We turned south for a bit, then east again for High Halden along the undulating and twisting Kentish roads to Great Chart and Ashford where we pulled into the Saracen's Head to rest the horses while we had lunch. This hotel stood on the north-west corner of North Street and High Street and was pulled down some ten or twelve years ago. After a leisurely lunch we clambered aboard and left again, going along the Stour valley through Godmersham, past Chilham on its hill, along Win-

John, Borys, Joseph Conrad and J. B. Pinker in front of Oswalds, 1921

cheap, round the city wall into St George's Place and along the Dover road, past the Gate Inn and down into Bridge. We turned right just after the church through Bourne Park to Bishopsbourne and Oswalds.

The stables had been cleaned out and fresh straw laid in the stalls, the other half of the garage had been cleaned out and all the old junk removed in readiness for the coach. The horses were rested the next day and the coach was washed and leathered; the whole harness was attended to and all the metal work and glass cleaned and polished until it shone like new. It took almost the whole day to do but the next day was the first day of cricket and we were all going.

The following morning, Saturday, there was great activity getting the coach ready, harnessing the horses, preparing the lunch-basket and putting all the various bits and pieces into the coach, as we were to spend the whole day at the ground. We arrived before play commenced and parked the coach by the raised bank on the south side of the ground from where we had a good view of the pitch. The arrival of the coach created quite a stir among the people who had come to watch the cricket and for a time there was a steady stream of sightseers. JC found this rather trying and after a bit asked me to walk with him round the ground, stopping every now and again to talk to acquaintances. JC treated everyone with courtesy, asking after their health and their family, whoever they were.

We watched the play during the morning but I could see that my father found it boring, no one wanted to talk and apart from the occasional gasp at a missed catch there was silence. When we had finished lunch, which had been al fresco, the lunch-basket was taken to the car and JC took the opportunity to go home and back to a more civilised atmosphere. On the Monday the coach took the enthusiasts to the cricket but JC remained at home saying that he might come later when the car came in, but I had my doubts and no one was really surprised when the car arrived without him.

The following day the horses needed to be exercised so instructions were given for the coach to be ready at two o'clock for a country drive. My mother's leg made it impossible for her to get into or onto the coach so Mrs Pinker decided to stay and keep her company while the rest of us rolled along the Kentish lanes. We went up the hill over the Dover road and through the lanes to join the road to Sandwich at Bramling. We passed through Wingham and Ash and were crossing the flat marshland about a mile from Sandwich when, after a long silence on the part of the passengers, JB announced that he would describe how he was driving the four horses. This 'running commentary' would have been interesting if any of us had been aspiring coach-drivers but it left my father and me rather bored and the rest found it somewhat embarrassing.

'Now I must swing wide to take this corner, so I draw the nearside leader over to the centre before I get there and then I draw the offside leader over as we go through the bend. I pull on all four horses to stop – what's that silly fellow doing in the middle of the road – oh, taking a photograph – he ought to stay on the pavement. Now we drop to a walk as we have to make a sharp turn to the right – straight out and now draw on the off leader and we – are – round. Conrad, you will have to pilot me through the town.'

I could tell that my father had found the commentary more than a little irritating and we were both glad when it ceased. JC was sitting on JB's left and I was sitting behind JB so my father had only to look over his shoulder to see me. He glanced round with rather a bored look and, was that just the suspicion of a wink? I was not sure at the time. Mr Pinker had got the horses going again at a brisk trot since there was practically no traffic to speak of, and we were bowling along round a slight bend when JC said,

'Take the next left – if you can!' As soon as he spoke I knew he was wrong and even if he had not been he had left it a bit late, but JB managed to get us round without mounting the offside pavement. 'Hey, whoa there, whoa, steady now, whoa!' and we came to standstill, JB very angry.

'I asked to be piloted through the town not into a cul-de-sac. Really you ought to know your way around by now. Just as well I know what to do!' Turning to the coachmen he said:

'We'll have to take the leaders off and work our way round. I think there is enough room.' It took a little while to unhitch the horses and lead them away towards the end of the street and then everyone had to get off the coach except JB and the turning operation commenced.

JC watched while I gave a hand, pushing and pulling amid an awful lot of fuss, far more than either of us felt was necessary, and JC remarked: 'There is nothing like making a fuss to impress people if you're not quite sure of how to do a thing.' At last the outfit was turned round and the leaders hitched on again and we were told to get up onto our seats. JC got up beside me as there was a certain frigidity in the atmosphere and we quietly drew one another's attention to things of interest. We arrived in Deal and drove along the front but there was very little to see in the Downs apart from a couple of barges beating down Channel. After a stop to rest the horses we returned home through Mongeham, Eythorne and Shepherdswell. My father's only remark when we got home was:

'The countryside seemed lazy this afternoon, turning round much more slowly than when we are in the car. Of course sitting so much higher makes a difference. Still I'm glad that's over aren't you?' I agreed with him.

Everyone, with the exception of my parents, went to the remaining days of cricket, although JC was persuaded to come with us on the Thursday, Ladies' Day, as it was considered a social occasion.

Sunday morning came and the coach was brought round to the front door for the last time, the cases were stowed and the Pinker family said 'goodbye' and clambered aboard. Then with the horn sounding, they turned out of Oswalds drive and started on their journey home. My father and I agreed that it had been quite a pleasant experience but we were both glad that our usual form of travel was by car rather than by a horse-drawn vehicle.

Many people in all walks of life have remarked to me that my father always knew what he wanted without any indecision. His ability to get alongside a person was always a source of wonder and comment, particularly from those meeting him for the first time. Luther Milward, for whom JC had a high regard, in spite of their lengthy arguments, summed up the opinion of many when he said:

'Your Dad was a proper gentleman. He'd talk to you, not over your head or at you. He was always ready to learn and respect you and your opinions.'

I suppose I must have been aware of this ease of approach even in Aldington days when he talked to Slingsby but I did not really appreciate it until we moved to Oswalds. He took a great deal of interest in the well-being of those about him, but not ostentatiously. He had an uncanny instinct for finding the right person to ask for information and because he respected their confidences they talked freely to him and no one ever thought that he was being 'nosey'.

His courtesy and manners were always remarked upon, especially by the wives of friends and neighbours; many a time have I been greeted by elderly ladies, 'How do you do? I hope you have managed to learn some of your father's perfect manners!' It took some living up to but I tried. Of course there were times when his politeness was misunderstood. I remember being told of the time when we had advertised for a housemaid and it had been arranged that she should come to be interviewed by my mother and, rather typically, my father had not been told. JC was crossing the hall when the doorbell rang and so he opened the door and saw a young woman standing there: 'Belle visage – très chic' – brought his heels together with a click, bowed from the hips and asked her in. She seemed a bit nervous so he took her hand and raised it to his lips, making her even more nervous. Then after hesitating a moment she turned and fled down the drive, much to JC's bewilderment. After explanations he observed that, perhaps, it was as well that she took fright if she did not appreciate normal, polite behaviour.

19

Missing tools – aversion to police – lost tool case –
lost stick – the thief spotted – bread pellets –
drawings – Rothenstein – flying around

Our peaceful existence continued except for some slight ripples on
the otherwise calm surface caused by the mysterious disappearance
of tools from the garage and engine room. As long as one took care to
put things fairly high up, on a bench or window cill they did not seem
to go missing quite so often. One could not help being a bit surprised
by the sudden appearance of a spanner in the middle of the yard that
had been devoid of any such thing seconds before. It kept happening,
but the crew took care not to spread the news around though they let
me into their confidence since I had lost a number of things. I
mentioned to my mother that tools were still being lost and we
discussed the idea of asking the police to help, but decided to delay
such drastic action.

My father had a very strong aversion to policemen in uniform and
if one came to the door he would shut himself in his study and refuse
to come out. At first I was amused until I realised the reason for this
behaviour: my father and his parents had every cause to distrust
officers of the law in those unhappy days when my grandparents
were ruthlessly deported to Siberia by the Russians. When our
village policeman came to collect a donation for a police charity or
sell tickets for their sports he always came as a private individual
during his off-duty time. He would be taken to the study, given a
glass of beer and a cheque and stay for fifteen to twenty minutes
talking to JC. If he met my father when he was on duty he would
touch his helmet but never stop to talk and my father would smile as
he walked straight past him.

One morning a catastrophe occurred. Vinten had been handed a
new set of car tools in a case that he had unwrapped and laid on the
running-board while he opened the bonnet of the car. When next he

looked, the wrapping was there, but not a sign of the tools or the case. We searched everywhere, but there was not a trace. He asked me to stay by the car to see that nothing was disturbed while he went with some trepidation to fetch my father. JC took it very calmly and surveyed the scene of the disappearance while I sat on the running-board patting the dog, Scallywag. JC looked all round and satisfied himself that there were no tools or case, he opened the door and looked under the seats and as he turned away Scally jumped up and settled himself on the seat. JC patted the dog and told Vinten to order another set of tools and to keep an eye open for any sign of the ones that had vanished.

A few days later Vinten came up to my room to ask why I had taken a hammer from the engine room. I denied even having seen the hammer, let alone taken it.

'Well, how do you explain my sister, Edith, finding it on the floor of the passage just outside this room this morning?' I repeated that I had not taken it and had no idea how it got there.

I told my parents about it at lunchtime and JC said that 'this damned nonsense has got to stop'. How? No one had any suggestion that made sense.

After lunch I went back to my room to carry on with what I had been doing, when I heard JC approaching along the passage and I could tell that he was not at all pleased.

'Hey, have you seen my stick?'

'No, it was on the chair in the hall after lunch.'

'Yes, I know but now it cannot be found.'

I went down to the hall with him and we searched everywhere but there was no sign of the stick. JC was furious, 'Why can't people keep their damned hands off my property?' I returned to my room and stood looking down into the yard. There was a light on in the engine room and I wondered what Vinten was doing. I was on the point of turning away when I saw Scally, with something in his mouth, poke his head round the doorpost, look both ways, then trot off towards the garden. I watched to see where he was going but lost sight of him behind the hedge. I leant out of the window and saw Burchett, the gardener, coming from the direction that the dog had taken. I called to him to ask if he had seen the dog but he had not, so Scally must have turned down the path to the Dutch Garden where the other gardener was working. I went down and out into the garden and asked Louis Ford if he had seen the dog, but he had not noticed him.

This was getting beyond a joke. The dog had come out of the engine room with what looked like a spanner in his mouth and trotted off towards the kitchen garden and vanished. I liked conjuring tricks but this was a bit too much. All sorts of ideas were passing through my mind when suddenly I saw Scally snuffling in the roots of the hedge on the left of the path. He saw me and came to be patted with much wagging of the tail. It suddenly dawned on me who the culprit might be and the lump of damp earth on the tip of his nose tended to confirm my suspicions. I kept him near me as I walked round to the engine room yard where I could hear a heated argument in progress.

'But Charlie, I tell you I have not taken your blessed spanner. What would I want it for anyway?'

'Look, it was lying there by the mat and I only went to get the pliers from next door and it has gone. No one else has been along here so where is it?' As I arrived they both turned to me,

'Have you seen the adjustable wrench?'

'Yes, I've seen it. The dog took it down the garden and buried it.'

'Now, look, don't try and be funny. We've got work to do.'

'Come on follow me.' Then taking a firm hold of the dog's collar I led them down the path for a few paces then turned into a gap in the hedge where I had seen the dog emerge. Scally drew back and slipped his collar and disappeared at high speed. We went into the space behind the hedge and there we saw about half a dozen mounds a bit larger than molehills and one of them appeared to have freshly turned earth on it. We raked the soil aside and there was JC's walking-stick, the wrench and the case of tools; and when we opened up the other mounds we found all the things that had gone missing over the past months.

I took JC his stick and told him that all the lost tools had been found. JC said, 'I was going to ask you to keep an eye on that dog. His behaviour is much too like that of the Chinaman who stole all my money. All smiles to your face but snatch anything behind your back. We'll have to find another home for that dog.' Later on JC had a visit from Vinten and Foote to ask whether the dog might stay if they could cure him of pinching tools. My father gave them a fortnight to break Scally of his thieving habits and they succeeded except for one thing; he still persisted in burying his bones in the kitchen garden. However after a few more weeks he was taught to bury his bones in a piece of waste ground by the garage.

My father had a trick at meal-times when he was annoyed of

taking a little pinch of bread and flicking it about the room at random. At home it did not matter so much, but it could be rather embarrassing when he did it in a restaurant – some diner sitting at a distant table would jump when a pellet landed in the soup or hit him in the face or on the neck. He tried to overcome this habit and had succeeded when away from home though it still happened occasionally in our own dining room and, I suppose it was only to be expected, I copied him with disastrous results. I made a very good shot, in my own opinion, and hit Arthur Foote, our butler, straight in the eye, just as he was handing a dish of cauliflower-au-gratin to my father. JC did not say a word as the dish landed on his lap but got up and went upstairs to change. He came down again and called me into the hall where he proceeded to give me a well-deserved 'dressing-down' – I never tried experimenting with bread pellets after that.

Often my father asked me to make him a drawing, not just to keep me busy, but because he really wanted some picture or part of it enlarged. One particular drawing I made for him was of the family crest, with the two crests from which it derived on either side. It took a considerable time to enlarge it to the size he wanted – chiefly on account of the scrolls, which were most elaborate. After I had made the line drawings to his satisfaction I spent a whole afternoon mixing paints under his direction so that the colours would be correct. He kept this drawing in his desk and I was to have put it in a frame for him during the summer holidays of 1924, but it was lost or acquired by someone when his papers were being sorted after his death, after having been in the drawer for over two years.

The only drawing I did for my father of which there are copies in existence is the family crest which appears on the inside of the front cover of the Hour Glass Edition of 1923 published by J. M. Dent and Sons. I remember being called to the study and asked to make a drawing as a 'purely commercial deal for an agreed charge of half a guinea'.

It was not often that I tried to make sketches in the house or garden, at that time I looked upon such activities as being more in keeping with schooldays than 'home' days, but there was one occasion when the Rothensteins were staying with us. Perhaps I was trying to attract attention: I don't know; but I was seated by the inner garden door trying to make a drawing of the staircase and hall and very intent on what I was doing. I had drawn in and rubbed out one part as I could not get it to look right when I realised that Will

Rothenstein was looking over my shoulder. I appealed to him to help me but he told me to go on trying as I would learn far more if I found out for myself. His only advice was that the underside of the stairs had a different vanishing point from the walls and floor because of its slope and that a softer pencil was easier to rub out. I was disappointed at the time though I came to appreciate his advice later on. It struck me as strange that JC rarely talked about pictures or drawings, because he seemed to have a natural gift for drawing as well as a keen interest in geometry and algebra. He had a remarkable sense of proportion and his drawings of ships were very good in spite of the fact that he used a matchstick dipped in ink for their creation.

I suppose I should not have been surprised at the fuss my father made when he was going on a journey or to stay with friends. Several days before he was due to leave he would start fussing about clothes and suitcases – the latter had to be clean but the labels of previous trips were not to be removed. As captain or first officer of a sailing ship he would have stowed his personal belongings some days before the ship was due to sail. He would 'fly round' (his pet expression) to get everything in order so that he could give his undivided attention to getting under way. He would allow nothing to interfere with his preparations and as Captain Hope once said to me with a laugh, 'The ship is more important to your father than his safety or his life.'

20

Welsh trip – change of car – Daimler – chess –
Northcliffe – Zagorska – Graham – billiards – Curle

It was in the summer of 1922 that my parents and I were invited to
go for a tour of Wales with Sir Robert Jones and his son-in-law
Frederick Watson. We arrived at Lime Street station in Liverpool
towards evening and were met by Sir Robert's car and taken to
Belvedere Road. My memories are a bit hazy but I remember
looking up a staircase as we entered the hall, and wondering what my
room would be like in this tall town-house on the outskirts of Liverpool. There was an immense drawing room, very lofty, full of furniture and on one side the very latest in musical reproduction, an
enormous panatrope, which was an early type of large cabinet
gramophone. The record and pickup were covered by a lid, the front
had two or three 'fretted' openings with a panel of frosted glass in the
centre. Behind this glass were a number of coloured electric lights
which were switched on and off by 'the music', so I was told at the
time. I have a suspicion that it was the intensity of the sound rather
than the notes which caused a sort of miniature aurora borealis to
appear on the frosted glass.

After dinner Sir Robert put on a number of records for our
entertainment and we sat listening to the music against a background of needle hiss. They were mostly orchestral pieces at almost
full volume to reduce the hiss and, I very much suspect, to preclude
any conversation, but my mother and Sir Robert seemed to like the
noise though JC and I found it rather trying. For those days the
reproduction was very good but too loud for comfort and as soon as
good manners allowed I retired to bed pleading tiredness after the
train journey from Kent. Next morning JC came to my room to see if
I was getting up. He knocked on the door and came in and as I was
almost dressed he sat on the bed to wait for me while I finished
packing.

'Well, what do you think of the latest in musical boxes?'

'There was too much noise for the size of the room – I felt overpowered by it.'

'Yes, we were too tired to enjoy it and anyhow one should go to a concert hall to hear music in its right environment. There is too much distraction in a house especially when it is someone else's. Thank heavens we cannot take it with us, eh?'

I could see that my father was finding the whole affair rather irritating and he was glad when Mr Watson arrived for the beginning of our tour. Sir Robert and my mother were to travel in a large Armstrong Siddley limousine while my father was to go with Mr Watson in his Rover Tourer and I was left to choose which car I would travel in. I chose the Armstrong Siddley and got up beside the chauffeur, but I rather regretted my choice after a few miles. The seat was incredibly uncomfortable and the car behaved like a wayward tank. If one got too near the verge it tried to go into the ditch, and if one got onto a patch of wet road it was practically uncontrollable. Luckily the driver, previously the coachman, kept the speed down to a very sedate thirty miles an hour, crawling past other traffic, creeping round corners. Since there was very little traffic I did not think we would come to much harm. We crossed over the Mersey by the ferry to Birkenhead and here the Rover left us to pursue our stately way over the Dee at Queensferry, on to Mold and over the high ground to Ruthin where we stopped for lunch.

After lunch I asked if I could ride in the back of the Rover with Mr Watson and JC. We headed north-east for Denbigh and up over the moor to Bylchau where we turned left for Pentre–Feolas, then right for Betws-y-Coed where we were to spend the night. JC enjoyed the drive but was disappointed by the lack of distance in the view. He turned to me as we topped a low pass with the remark, 'Now, we should see a stretch of country' but when we got over the crest there was another one ahead. After this had happened four or five times my father asked Mr Watson, 'Is this dammed country never going to show itself to us?' However later in the afternoon he was appeased by wider views and a straight length of road where Mr Watson let the Rover out and we touched nearly sixty miles an hour. JC was delighted as he liked travelling fast. We had to start slowing down some distance before the end of the straight section and JC was quite put out because Mr Watson had 'not used all the road'. I could not hear their conversation without leaning forward but I was quite content to watch the countryside spin by. We arrived at the Hotel at Betws-y-Coed about teatime and JC enjoyed the peace and quiet of a sunny evening in the mountains.

Next morning we left about ten o'clock, retracing our road of the previous day and then going on to Corwen and Llangollen before turning south for Oswestry and then southwest for Llanfechain where we stayed with Mr and Mrs Watson for a few days before returning to Oswalds.

Soon after we returned it was suggested by Mrs C that we should change the open Cadillac for a closed car; she had found Sir Robert's limousine far more comfortable and less tiring when she was not buffeted by the wind. The hood and side screens of the Cadillac let in a lot of wind and rain and were due for renewal in any case. After some searching, another Cadillac with a Cabriolet-de-Ville body was found, a masterpiece of massive construction. The previous car was heavy but the replacement was even heavier, and I am pretty sure was built by a waggonbuilder rather than a coachbuilder. The workmanship was good but the detailed design lacked refinement though it kept out the wind and rain. It was a poor affair and started to give trouble as soon as we got it – the mudwings of quarter inch thick aluminium on iron brackets fell off in rotation, while the doors needed constant attention to make them shut and stay shut. It was not surprising that before long we cast around for something better.

My brother was working in London at the time and managed to get a 38 horse-power Daimler Landaulet, a magnificent vehicle with royal antecedents. It is a fact that when it was delivered it had a royal coat of arms on the doors and my father refused to ride in it until the crests had been painted over. It was beautifully finished and equipped. It had massive brass lamps which we managed to convert to electricity without destroying their appearance. It was very comfortable for my mother, and relatively easy to get into and there was a really amazing amount of room for four people in the back. The rear part of the hood was made of leather and could be folded down in warm weather.

The months passed and the Christmas holidays came and went without disturbing the peaceful tenor of our life. Our games of chess began soon after supper, sometimes going on into the early hours of the morning as we were more closely matched now and the games became more and more absorbing. My father no longer came to my room in the small hours to get me to come down for a game as he had done.

Lord Northcliffe's friendship with my father continued and he was always very generously disposed towards me and my father did not begrudge this attention. JC seemed to have overcome his jealousy or anxiety when I was with his friends with the possible exception of Richard Curle; certainly he did not fuss as much as he used to when I was younger. My first wireless-set was give to me by Lord Northcliffe, a cat's-whisker crystal set with headphones which he insisted in setting up himself in my playroom over the kitchen after he had supervised the erection of the aerial. Though I was grateful for the gift I was not very interested in the wireless and JC was very disappointed with it. Whenever I got a signal and took off the headphones to hand to him it would fade or start crackling or if he could hear voices someone would shut a door with unnecessary violence and upset the tuning.

Our Polish cousin, Karola Zagorska, came to stay and we became close friends but not until I got used to her trick of gazing at one in silence. So intense was her concentration at the time that one had to pat her on the shoulder to get an answer to a question. She practised singing every morning in the drawing room and it was my job to see that Scally, the dog, was kept well away as he would persist in trying

Daimler, 38 horse power, ex-royalty

to join in. He would snuffle along the bottom of the drawing-room door making little grunting noises rather than whining; it was a cheerful noise, and in no way sorrowful but very distracting for anyone trying to sing. Karola and my father always spoke Polish and occasionally French though they were both quite capable of speaking in English. This used to upset Mrs C sometimes and then Karola had to make a fuss of her to restore her usual good humour. Later on Karola went to America where she became an opera singer but after the Second World War she returned to England, on her way back to Poland. Unfortunately we did not hear of her arrival in time to try to persuade her not to go on to Poland. We never heard from her or from her sister, Aniela, again.

There was a fairly steady flow of visitors to Oswalds, either for lunch, for the day or for a week-end. As I have mentioned before JC's particular friends, Cunninghame Graham, Garnett and Curle nearly always came alone. It was so much easier for JC to have only one guest, and the possibility of creating misunderstandings between them was removed. Mrs Dummett often came with Don Roberto for lunch, always beautifully dressed and 'chic'. She was a brilliant conversationalist in a variety of languages who went out of her way to translate anything in a foreign tongue so that my mother could understand. I do not recall that they ever stayed the night whereas Curle and Garnett nearly always did. Jean Aubry came but, after one shattering week-end when Richard Curle was staying as well, he too used to come alone. They did not get on together at all, Jean had no sense of humour and was inclined to take offence at the slightest opportunity and retire to his room. I have no idea what the row was about, but after it they would not meet again.

Cunninghame Graham was a close but not intimate friend of my father: not intimate in the sense that JC did not discuss with him the family fortunes or problems. In later years he became a valued and trusted friend of mine as I grew up; though he was always friendly he never overdid his attention to me, but 'let me be' before we tired of each other's company.

My father held him in high regard and whilst respecting his political views was not above chaffing him when opportunity arose, and JC never took umbrage if Don Roberto repeated a word to show my father that his pronunciation was not quite what it should have been. Their sense of humour was very similar and they often enjoyed a good laugh together. When he came to Oswalds he always found time to spend with my mother and made a point of having a quiet chat with me usually about my parents' health but more particularly about my father's. If he had arranged to meet my father in London he would make me responsible for seeing that the meeting took place. My father was still just a trifle jealous of Don Roberto's attention to me and, to a lesser extent, to Mrs C, though she could not take Don Roberto out of sight on account of her lameness. When he came with me down to the village or across the park we would vanish into thin air to JC's anxiety and we would find him on the 'look out' for us when we returned. Don Roberto enjoyed walking and often remarked that he would like JC to come, but my father had no inclination to walk in the country, he preferred to stroll in the garden or walk slowly to visit a neighbour. Looking back one cannot help thinking that he would have been less of an invalid if he had lived in a drier situation or, perhaps, by the sea where he always seemed to feel better.

As I grew up I seemed to drift further away from Edward Garnett and I have the impression that the friendship between JC and Uncle Edward was not as close as it had been. He was quite friendly, but somehow, it could have been my absence at school, our early 'rapport' diminished and I saw less and less of him when we moved to Oswalds.

It would be fair to say that as 'JC's friendship with Garnett diminished, so that with Curle increased, though the friendships themselves were of a different nature. Whilst Garnett's friendship was based on his advice as a reader, Curle's friendship had a much broader base; his keen observation on his travels, his ability to create a word-picture of a place or situation was always a source of delight to my father. It was a profound friendship outside the knowledge and appreciation of practically everyone, even of those other friends who witnessed it. Dick, as we all called him, became part of the family and was a frequent and very welcome visitor whenever he was in England.

We had a quarter-size billiard table which was put onto an old kitchen table in the den when we wanted to play, and JC usually had a game with Dick when he came to stay. It was played at a very leisurely tempo almost as though it was more important to fill up time rather than play the game. It was my job to score but I must admit I yawned a lot. However to make up for my boredom Dick performed various tricks: balancing a cue on the toe of his shoe, or going out into the stairwell to balance it on the tip of his nose. He was very good at all the different tricks and JC thoroughly enjoyed the performance.

There is no doubt whatever that Dick became my father's closest friend and they were at peace with one another, in complete harmony even when silence reigned during a break in conversation. On those rare occasions when I joined them in the study I was aware of the atmosphere of complete confidence between them. It was uncanny how their thoughts seemed to proceed on parallel lines and I was amazed how, after a long silence, one of them would respond to a comment by the other in such a way as to make it seem that there had been no period of silence. Several times I noticed how one of them would pick up a conversation which they had left unfinished the evening before without having to refresh the other's mind. They were both men of great perception but even so it seems to me to have been quite remarkable.

I know that Dick always looked forward to visiting us and my father was always concerned to see that his visit should be restful and happy. JC took a personal interest and would go up to the spare room with Foote to see that everything was provided that Dick could possibly need – books, cigarettes, ashtrays, matches and whisky and soda. He would tell Foote that Mr Curle was to have everything that was required and 'see that he gets it before he asks for it'. No one else, outside the family, had as much fuss made about his visit and I am sure my father only did it to show in a material way how much he enjoyed Richard Curle's company.

Dick had travelled in the East and knew many of the places that my father had visited, so they had an unlimited stock of memories to draw upon and as they were both extremely observant there was never any lack of material or subject about which to talk. JC's observations seemed to me to be more concerned with man's creative efforts – ships, houses, bridges, and things made by man – while Dick's were more interested in nature, birds, insects and in the human race which of course provided unlimited scope for discussion. JC became noticeably elated as the time approached for Dick's arrival and continued to be so for a few days after he had left though my father was always a little depressed at the time of parting. Dick's visits invariably stimulated my father though, to be fair, the visits of Cunninghame Graham and Garnett also did but in a subtly different way. Conversation, argument, or story-telling, seemed almost like

Richard Curle at Oswalds, 1923

an 'elixir vitae' to him; he enjoyed talking to Baker at Deal, or Milward, just as much as to a learned professor.

My father was known to his friends for his extravagant generosity but none of them received quite so much personal attention as Richard Curle. JC's directness of approach, lack of conceit and genuine delight at meeting friends dispelled any feelings of jealousy between them though while we lived at Capel House some acquaintances showed signs of envy.

Scallywag, the dog, was as delighted to see Dick as the rest of us, and JC often observed 'that dog will snap in half if he wags his tail so much'. The dog seemed to know when Dick was coming and would lie in wait in the hall for his arrival. I remember once, when I had been with Vinten to fetch Dick from the station I heard the dog whining and snuffling on the other side of the front door. As I opened it to let Dick in, Scally leapt up at him, pushing him very firmly onto a chair by the side of the door. My father came out of the study and seeing Dick seated on the chair, pushing the dog away said: 'Good God, Dick what has happened? Are you ill?'

Dick had been winded by the dog who was still fussing round him and JC told me that he was to be kept tied up for the rest of Dick's stay, but it was not long before I was told to let him loose again. Dick often asked me, 'Do you think that that dog is really as pleased to see me as he appears to be? Look at him now wagging his whole body to and fro.' I assured Dick that the dog only made all that fuss for him alone, but it was a difficult question to answer with certainty. After all it is the person who is being fussed who knows, or should do.

If Dick came to stay when the fruit was ripe we'd go down the garden before breakfast and help ourselves to peaches and nectarines, as he maintained that the only way to enjoy the fruit was to pick it and eat it while it was still warm from the sun. No doubt he was right but the gardeners were more than a bit put out and did not fail to let me know it!

Richard Curle and Sir Ralph Wedgwood had been close friends for some time and it was only natural that JC should ask them to act as trustees and take control of the estate. Dick, in the twelve years that he had known the family, had learnt a lot about us and I think it was only because of his regard for JC that he agreed to become a trustee. I often thought that his friendship was taxed to the limit and sometimes abused by the frequent and thoughtless demands made upon it during the first few years after my father's death. True we had often entertained him but he more than repaid any debt that may have been incurred by the unselfish attention he gave to my mother in various ways. He carried through numerous financial deals with the help of Mr Tom Withers when my mother changed houses, which was pretty often. He had a rather thankless task, so it seemed to me, but in spite of many vicissitudes he administered affairs wisely and surely and eventually handed over the literary estate to the family solicitors, Messrs Withers, and myself in 1944.

More than once he had to read the riot act but his judgement was sound and he had the full support of Sir Ralph Wedgewood and the solicitors. He gave me a lot of prudent advice, the greater part of which I acted upon but there were those occasions when I upset him by some remark which, unintentionally, caused a misunderstanding, though on the whole, these periods did not last long I am happy to say.

There was a friend of my father's who wrote or sent telegrams asking for urgent financial assistance, and one of these demands arrived while Dick was staying with us. It was due to him that my father, instead of sending the amount asked for, sent only a small percentage of it. I can still hear Dick's voice saying

'Conrad, is this man very important to you? Does his friendship mean a lot? Is it really necessary to send any money? Just send him ten pounds or something like that. He seems to be a hopeless beggar from what you have told me.'

'Well − he is in trouble—'

'All right, he's in trouble so he ought to get out of trouble or not get into it in the first place. You can't go on supporting these odd people who seem to think that you are made of money − it isn't right.'

JC accepted Dick's advice and was grateful for it as it saved quite an appreciable amount. My father was inclined to be too generous, particularly to tramps and people down on their luck.

Returning from the station after I had seen Dick off, one day, I was called into the study by JC who asked,

'Have you seen our honoured guest safely aboard the train?'

'Yes, I have. We had to wait a short while.'

'He is an honoured guest, you know. He's got a "long head" on those shoulders; a wise man. Listen well to his counsels.'

Dick Curle became as close a friend of mine as he had been of JC but the friendship was not as 'complete', the difference in our ages and interests made that impossible, though he never treated me as anyone but an equal, even when I was being a bit 'mulish'. He often came to stay with my wife and me after we were married and his visits were looked forward to by our two boys. He and I would talk far into the night about my father, or my work or about the people he met when staying with us.

2 I

Walpole – hypocrisy – dislike of Russians –
Goodburn – Epstein – Powell – Tittle – Aubry – Le
Havre – Gide – Aubry's parents – Bost family

Hugh Walpole was a fairly regular visitor to Oswalds and usually arrived all smiles and friendliness. He spent more time with my mother than other friends who came, but he never became a really close friend. JC liked having him to stay now and again as he was a fairly easy person to talk to, a bit inclined to gossip, which JC didn't approve of and there was a noticeable lack of 'fussing' on my father's part when he came.

Once he arrived in a great state of enthusiasm when JC and I were waiting at the front door for the car to arrive. He was hardly in the house before he said, thrusting a book at my father: 'Conrad, Conrad, I have here a most excellent dictionary, quite the latest and best and it is for you.'

JC took the book, flicked through the pages and handed it to me, turned on his heel and led the way into the study as Walpole and I followed him. JC turned and looked at him, then said, 'You know, Hugh, I can spell and I can understand English. I may not always speak it very well but I have no need of a dictionary.'

Another time Walpole arrived and was met by the dog who jumped up and left two muddy paw marks on Hugh's immaculate trousers. He pushed the dog away saying, 'Christ, what a dammed mess you've made, blast you.'

My father, coming from the study, heard his remark and said, 'Hugh, you will keep your profanities for elsewhere. I won't have them in my house, please remember.' Walpole apologised but the next twenty-four hours were decidedly chilly and JC did not forgive him until next afternoon.

He became 'Uncle' Hugh though he was never more than just

friendly, hardly ever attempting conversation with me but I did not mind particularly. My father's friends fitted into pigeon holes in my mind and I knew what to expect when each one came, when to make myself scarce and when not to. I never joined Walpole in the study after dinner as I realised from the dinner-table conversation that it would be of no interest to me.

It was strange to see how people got the 'wrong' idea of my father, a completely erroneous idea that he was 'a man eater', a concept usually held by people who should have known better. I have often wondered why – even my brother referred to him on one occasion as 'a very furious man' and I believe it may have been due to two furrows above the bridge of the nose giving the impression of a perpetual frown. This could be the reason for some people remarking to me after meeting him that he was not nearly so fierce as they thought he might be.

This facial feature, which shows in nearly every photograph of my father, could have been in the mind of a reporter who came to interview JC and who started off badly by trying to cover his in-experience by the 'gushing torrent' approach, 'Oh, Mr Conrad, I am so sorry but I have not read any of your books, terribly wrong of me to come and bother you like this when I am so ignorant about your books—.' All said at high speed and completely lacking any sincerity.

JC looked at him, 'Sir, you are a hypocrite. I don't blame you for not reading my books but don't come here pretending you are terribly sorry because you do not give a damn whether you have read them or not.' JC's ability for sizing up people or their intentions could be quite disconcerting and he always knew a 'scallywag' when he saw one.

On another occasion a young reporter turned up and barged into the house when the maid opened the door, and stalked into the study without waiting to be announced. He left his hat, coat and case on the chair by the door and without introducing himself said, 'Now, sir, you're a Russian of course—.' He could not have said anything more likely to cause an explosion. JC came round the table, took him by the shoulders, spun him round and hustled him along the short passage to the front door which he opened, pushed him outside and slammed the door. Then he saw the man's hat on the chair by the door. He opened the door again and threw the hat out, slammed the door, then saw the coat and case and repeated the operation. In the end the reporter was left standing in the drive, his hat at his feet, his coat and case a bit further away, wondering what on earth he had said to cause such a reaction. He waited a short while and then took himself off, he did have the grace not to try and 'cook up' a report on an interview which did not take place. At the time his enforced departure amused me, but then I knew the reason for it – someone ought to have explained it to him.

My father's dislike of Russians was very understandable and on one occasion caused considerable embarrassment to a friend who had not bothered to find out whether my father would lunch with a Russian. JC spotted the Russian as soon as he entered the room, turned on his heel and walked out and refused to speak to his host for a very long time afterwards. No one can blame him when one recalls the treatment they meted out to his parents.

My studies at school did not progress as well as they might have done, so during the holidays from 1921 onwards I had tuition each morning given me by Harold Goodburn. JC had a very high opinion of Goodburn and he helped me to improve my knowledge very considerably, as he had the knack of imparting knowledge and made every subject more interesting than most of the masters I had at school. He became a very close friend and remained so throughout his life. JC never 'badgered' me about my lack of achievement at school and when I did succeed in winning one or two prizes for drawing he gave me unstinted praise. He would have liked me to become a marine or civil engineer but at that time I was more interested in cars and engines.

Everyone was most careful not to make any remarks that might be misconstrued as being critical of him when Jean Aubry came. He was so serious, always on his dignity and prone to take umbrage at the least provocation and always impeccably attired, seemingly for ever flicking invisible specks of dust or hairs from his clothes. Occasionally he would smile at a joke but I do not remember ever seeing him laugh. This lack of humour and impatience when questioning people could well have been the reason for the somewhat 'dry' treatment of *The Life and Letters* which could have been so much more entertaining had he troubled to listen to friends who knew my father before he did.

I was at school when Jacob Epstein came to make a portrait bust of JC, which was just as well from what I heard afterwards and found in my room over the kitchen which had been 'used' as a studio. 'Used' was the operative word. There were lumps of clay and plaster all over the place, in the cupboards and on the picture rails and window cills and a drawing I had been preparing for JC was ruined where someone had tried to scoop off a lump of plaster and torn a piece right out. My comments were not printable and JC expressed himself forcibly about the behaviour of some people! I heard that Epstein was quite a difficult person to have about the house so it was as well that he and his wife and child had rooms in the White Lion Inn at Bridge. The atmosphere was quite tense enough without having them to stay in the house.

When John Powell, the American pianist, came to stay, I was at home and he played for us each evening when several friends came to listen. Someone suggested that the piano, a Broadwood Grand, should be turned so that the keyboard could be seen. Whether it was this turning or not a lot of the higher notes got 'lost' due to the extraordinary acoustics so the listeners only heard bits of the performance. When I suggested that there was something wrong with the sound Mr Powell assured my father that the piano was well tuned and in excellent order – 'acoustics' were not generally understood in those days!

Walter Tittle came to Oswalds to make drawings of my father before painting his portrait and I was allowed to sit and watch him at work. At the time I did not appreciate his patience in answering my questions but I was grateful for his comments and look back to that morning as one of the most instructive I have ever spent. His portrait of JC in the National Gallery is a good likeness. It is a little highly coloured and the hands appear a little 'clawlike' but this, I think, was to make them appear to be strong.

There were frequent unexpected events at Oswalds like the time an American couple turned up to interview my father for some periodical, and arrived at the front door towed by a large bulldog. They rang the bell and when Foote opened the door the husband was forcibly towed into the house by the dog, followed by his wife who was holding onto her husband's other hand with both of hers. There was quite a lot of noise and JC came out of the study to see what it was all about. Seeing the dog he said, 'Here, Foote, take his damned animal.'

As the leash was handed over the dog caught sight of a cat at the end of the hall. The dog, with Foote in tow on his posterior, disappeared down the hall at high speed, crashed into the folding glass doors, the leash broke and the animals vanished from sight down the garden. JC watched the episode and then turned to the American and his wife and said,

'And this I suppose is to facilitate our interview, eh?' He led them into the study where I have no doubt they spent an uncomfortable ten minutes before JC cooled down.

I left school at the end of the summer term of 1923 as JC had decided that I should spend some time in France learning the language. Jean Aubry, whose parents lived in Le Havre, had found a Protestant 'pasteur' who had young people to stay 'en pension', so we crossed from Southampton to make the necessary arrangements. We arrived very early in the morning and after 'petit déjeuner' at the Grand Hôtel, in the Place Gambetta, JC and I left my mother to unpack while we walked down 'Les Basins' and looked over the sailing ships tied up there. JC enjoyed the atmosphere of the port and hailed the men on board the various vessels. Now and again he would forget that I did not talk or understand French and be quite annoyed if I did not reply to a question.

After lunch we were joined by Jean Aubry and we piled into one of the taxis standing in front of Tortoni's restaurant and were taken to 19 Rue Mare where the Bost family lived. This was a tall three-storey house standing on a high bank of a walled plot of untended grass overlooking a quiet residential street about halfway up the hillside behind the town. It appeared to be rather a dismal place, paint peeling off the stucco, and the windows needing attention, but turned out to be a happy home for the Bost family of twelve and the four young students when I went to stay there.

We spent the afternoon there while JC arranged about my stay and Jean acted as interpreter for my mother and Madame Bost. My mother sat, apparently at ease, listening to them and occasionally making some remark which was translated. We sat in the 'salle à manger' so that my mother did not have to climb the stairs to the 'salon' on the first floor. Both these rooms faced south and were so very warm that I had quite a struggle to keep awake after our early arrival. At about half past three the 'pasteur' and JC joined us, and after a short while we took our leave and got into the taxi to be taken to Aubry's parents' flat, where we were to have tea. Here my mother had to climb the stairs to the first floor but the effort was worth it for her, because tea, apart from the drink which was welcome, was composed entirely of rich creamy cakes of all kinds which Mrs C thoroughly enjoyed. It was a cheerful place this flat of Papa and Mama Aubry as I found when I returned at the end of September.

The next day we had been invited to lunch by André Gide at his chateau at Gonneville-le-Mallet but my only recollection of that visit is being overloaded with Siamese cats as soon as I sat down. Gide had remembered my cats of Capel House days though I wished he had not – their talons were very sharp and my legs suffered as a consequence. Later that afternoon we went on to tea with the Bosts at Bruneval where they spent part of their holidays and, after another day in Le Havre, we returned home by the night packet.

22

Arrival in Le Havre – lunch at Gide's – Sheppard –
Sneller – doctor's locum – 3 August – Lyons –
funeral – a thought

Towards the end of September 1923 I left home to go to Le Havre to learn French and, as JC said, 'to widen my horizon'. I had never worried about being left to my own devices and was used to being on my own but leaving home for a foreign country was far more of a break than I had anticipated. I was not nearly so venturesome as my father had been but then I had had a happy home life and the need to get away was not great. I packed my bags in the afternoon and the car took me to the station for the late afternoon train to London where I boarded the nine o'clock boat-train for Southampton. I started off feeling important but that feeling had evaporated by the time I had found a seat in the restaurant-car and the thought crossed my mind that I would sooner be going home than across the Channel.

The train pulled into the platform at Southampton quayside where I was pounced on by a diminutive porter who recognised me from my previous trip and who steered me through and on board to the purser's office to book a cabin. I was very inexperienced and when he had seen me to my cabin I gave him ten bob as I had seen JC do. Needless to say he was 'my' porter from then on and he always met me at Southampton, when I crossed the Channel. As soon as we were clear of Spithead I went below and turned in but, after what seemed to me to be only a few minutes, I was awakened by the steward. I got dressed and had a cup of coffee and got back on deck just in time to see the ship tied up alongside the Quay. I went through customs, loaded my baggage onto a taxi and was driven to 19 Rue Mare where I arrived at about seven to find all the family busy about the house having already had their 'petit déjeuner'. The eldest daughter, Laly, showed me up to my room on the top floor from where I had a panoramic view of the whole town and estuary of the Seine. On one side of me was another Englishman, to be more correct a Scot, and on the other a very large young man from Alsace-Lorraine.

After I had unpacked I decided to pay my respects to Papa and Mama Aubry, and deliver a note that JC had asked me to give them. However before that I was shewn round the house and given a friendly lecture, in broken English, on the few simple rules I was expected to observe, so it was not until after 'déjeuner' that I was able to get away. My morning's instruction had been very complete, including very clear directions for getting down into the town by various short cuts so I found my way to the Aubrys' flat without any trouble. I was given tea, specially provided for me, and then Papa Aubry asked me to accompany him for his evening walk along the front up to Ste Addresse. On the way back he advised me to leave him and take the street by the Casino to my abode as it was nearing dinner time.

The Bosts were a most talented family, every member either played, or was learning to play, the piano and M. Le Pasteur was a locally well-known authority on the works of Bach. Every evening except Sundays they played 'a quatre mains' for two to three hours on the two pianos in the salon on the first floor, a long room stretching along the whole length of the front of the house although one end could be partitioned off.

Neither the Aubrys nor the Bosts spoke any English so I was obliged to get on with learning the language and fairly soon I could make myself understood. Madame Bost was a great help and frequently corrected my pronunciation though this sometimes led to long arguments with her husband as to what was correct. This was not helped by the sons and daughters who chimed in with their own versions. However the confusion that this caused was usually sorted out by Papa Aubry.

I came home for Christmas which passed in the usual peaceful manner and returned to Le Havre at the end of January 1924. As the weather improved I became more venturesome and went for long bicycle rides with Charlot Bost, the second son, over the countryside north of the town. When JC came over to arrange for my stay he had taken me to meet the British Consul and I spent many an evening in his company, sometimes at his flat at Ste Addresse, and sometimes driving out into the countryside to visit English families with whom he liked to keep in touch. When I went with him on these trips I had to make all the enquiries and find out where the people lived, which was all good practice.

On instructions from my father I asked M. Aubry if he could arrange for me to become a member of the fencing club and when I had been enrolled I used to accompany him each week for a lesson. I was by far the youngest member, all the others seemed to be well on in years but that did not prevent them from taking an afternoon's strenuous exercise. Unfortunately I could have only one lesson each week so my progress was rather slow, but I did improve gradually.

When we had visited Gide in 1923 he had asked me to visit him when I came over to stay so I wrote and asked when it would be convenient. He suggested that I should go over for lunch one day and so I set off one morning to cycle to Gonneville-le-Mallet. Once out of the town it is fairly flat rolling countryside but there was heatwave in progress and it was not long before I was perspiring freely and shedding bits of clothing in an endeavour to keep cool. I stopped by the entrance gates to put on my shirt and tie before going on to the chateau where he came out to meet me. He took me up to an enormous bathroom for a warm bath while my clothes were attended to, leaving me a voluminous bathrobe in which I wrapped myself before going down to the 'salon' for refreshments and a talk. After a short while a manservant came to say that my clothes were ready so I went and dressed and then we had lunch. After coffee I was shewn round the house and gardens and then I took my leave and cycled back to Le Havre.

Towards the end of June Mr Sheppard, the Consul, asked me to go with him to the southern part of his territory. I wrote to my father to ask his permission and I had a letter back by return, the gist of which was 'I sent you to France to learn the language and understand the French people so if you think that gallivanting about the countryside with an Englishman is going to make you understand the French more thoroughly I have no objection to your going. If on the other hand you are just going to watch the countryside whirl past you I strongly object but I leave it to your good sense to decide whether you are going to learn more or not.'

I showed the letter to Sheppard – 'We'll soon take care of that, I will take good care that you don't only look at the countryside, you will order the meals, buy the petrol, and attend to all the things we need on the journey, you will book the rooms at the hotels and see that we are not overcharged. In fact you will have to be a "complete Frenchman".' I agreed to try, but pointed out that I had yet to learn the more 'aggressive language' which I had heard used in some arguments.

We left Le Havre in the morning and took the riverside road to Caudebec where we crossed the river and then rolled on southwards through the Forêt-de-Brotonne and so to Conches for lunch. There were three of us as Mr Sheppard had brought a member of his staff to help him and to be a witness at any interviews that he might have. After we had studied the menu I was told to order lunch and I had understood that they wanted 'Escalop de veau'. Perhaps it was because I did not want to appear as an inexperienced traveller or, perhaps I was lazy, I only glanced down the menu, saw 'Esc...' pointed to it and asked for three portions. Imagine my consternation when instead of a dish of veal we were given a bowl of snails. I could not face them and said so in English only to be met by blank expressions on the faces of my companions. It was no use trying to find a hole into which to creep so I explained my mistake to the waiter and ordered afresh and managed to smile at my first 'faut pas'. After that I was much more careful and took my time even when we were short of time to study the menu carefully.

We proceeded south through Verneuil and La Loupe to Nogent-le-Rotrou where we stayed the night at the Hôtel du Dauphin. We left early in the morning for Bellême and Alençon making calls at each before going on to Flers where we were to spend the second night. Next day more calls were made on our homeward route, the last at about nine o'clock in the evening at Pont L'Eveque, finally getting back to Ste Addresse in the early hours of the morning.

For me it had been a tiring yet instructive trip and I wrote to tell JC all about it in my best French. A few days later I received a half sheet of notepaper thanking me and saying that my French was improving. Sheppard also had a letter from my father thanking him for his kindness and patience with 'my young scamp'.

Towards the end of July I packed my belongings so as to leave my room empty for another student who was coming for the summer holiday. At about half past ten in the evening I said my goodbyes and departed with my baggage in a taxi for the night crossing to Southampton. After watching the ship cast off I stayed on deck to watch the lights of Ste Addresse and Cap de la Hévè disappear into the night. I turned in but was roused in a very short time, so it seemed, by the steward with the information that the Home Fleet was at anchor off Spithead and that we would be going down the line of warships on our way into Southampton. What a chance! My camera clicked away until I had used up all the film. After going through customs, piloted by my diminutive porter, I found a seat in the restaurant-car for breakfast on the way to London. We pulled into Waterloo and I had ample time to go across for the train to Canterbury where I arrived about half past twelve to be met by Mr Sneller, our local taximan, who drove me home. Usually the car would have met me but I supposed that there was some good reason for its absence.

I found that Richard Curle was staying with us but the atmosphere was rather tense, which could not be entirely accounted for by my mother being confined to bed after another operation on her knee. I went up to her room as I usually did on my return home and she told me that JC was in bed having been taken ill suddenly when he was out in the car with Richard Curle earlier that morning. I went in to see him and realised that he was far from well but Dr Fox had been sent for and as we had a qualified nurse in the house I was not too worried.

I had been given the small bedroom next to the bathroom corridor, opposite my father's bedroom door, as Dick Curle had been put into my room over the kitchen. The spare room and what was called my brother's room had been set aside for him and his wife and small son who were due to arrive in the evening. Dr Fox was away so his locum had come over in his place and was shown upstairs as soon as he arrived. He spent some time with JC but was not worried by his condition when he came down; just saying that a few days in bed should see my father quite well again, but that he ought to have his teeth attended to as soon as could be arranged. Dick Curle spent part of the evening with him and I went in for a short while but he asked us to leave him as he did not want us to be upset when a spasm of breathlessness came upon him. I went and sat next door in my mother's bedroom with the rest of the family for a short while before going to bed.

It seemed that I had hardly fallen asleep before hurried footsteps in the passage outside woke me up. I heard Arthur Foote go along to my brother's bedroom, say something through the door and return to my father's room. There were more indistinct mutterings – then he came out and I was aware of him standing by the door as though

Joseph Conrad

waiting for something. I heard him start to go down the stairs, then I heard JC call out, very clearly, 'Here', followed by a confused noise of something sliding, then a thump, then silence.

I opened the door of my room and saw my brother and Foote go into JC's room, shutting the door behind them, and then became aware of my mother's voice asking what was the matter. My brother reappeared. 'Get dressed. Your father is dead.'

'Yes, I know.'

He did not wait but went into my mother's room. As I washed and dressed I heard Uncle Dick talking to Foote and then go into my father's room with him. Some time later, it may have been only a minute or so, I heard Uncle Dick talking to my mother and brother. I waited until he came out and then went in to see my mother. We looked at each other without a word and in silence I kissed her, still without speaking. I sat down by the fireplace. The silence pressed in on us, all-pervading, making movement a major effort and talking impossible. To me there was nothing, no feeling, no sound, nothing but a vast emptiness without features of any kind, yet all-enveloping. Uncle Dick looked in – 'Come and try to eat something.'

I went down the stairs in a sort of 'padded' atmosphere. All sounds seemed to be muted. I sat down at table oblivious of my surroundings – my brother came in and said, 'Reid is coming', turned, and went out again. Silence.

Douglas Reid had been my mother's doctor since we moved to Oswalds and he was the best person to comfort her at this hour. The empty hours passed through a soundless, shapeless void in silence. The whole household was stunned by the suddenness of it but the grief and emotion did not show until the next day.

Mr Lyons, brother of our faithful Nellie Lyons who had been with us for so many years at Capel until her death, arrived with the coffin which was carried up to my father's room. When it had disappeared I went up to sit with the rest of the family. We tried to pass the time and take our thoughts off the subdued sounds that could be heard from the next room. After what seemed a long time the sounds ceased and were followed by creaks from the staircase, while low voices faded away and silence flowed back into the house. I had not been so close to death before and it was the silence, almost tangible, that seemed to penetrate everywhere, which I noticed most.

In spite of only having just returned from the nursing home after another operation on her leg, indeed the wound was not completely healed, my mother insisted on coming downstairs and every morning, afternoon and evening she called me to go with her to look at my father lying in his coffin in the darkened drawing room. These visits were made in silence, not a word was spoken and after the first few visits not a tear was shed while we were together. After about two to three minutes she pressed my arm which she had held all the time and we would turn and go as silently as we had come. After the first few visits I looked across the coffin at the wall beyond – I wanted to remember JC as he was though he looked at peace with the world – he had made his 'last landfall'.

The day of the funeral dawned and friends started to arrive talking in subdued tones, casting sympathetic glances, but saying little, their hearts too full... The hearse arrived and Mr Lyons started the formalities for the last journey. It seemed natural that he should be there carrying on, in a sense, the attentions his sister had performed for so many years. He was no stranger to JC as he had often talked with him when he came to visit his sister at Capel House. He undertook all the arrangements, the cars to St Thomas's Church, and then on to the cemetery: down the length of the main street, round the Westgate Towers, up the Whitstable Road then left up the road to the entrance of the cemetery. The route was lined with people, mostly local, though with some visitors as it was cricket week. Here and there I caught the eye of a friend conveying silent sympathy and sorrow; my father had many friends in the city.

My mother did not attend the funeral. She would not have been able to walk the long way from the entrance to the grave nor could she have managed the service at St Thomas's Church.

My brother and his family returned to London while I stayed at home. I was coached by Harold Goodburn with the intention of going to Cambridge University, if I passed the entrance examinations, to study to become an engineer as had been my father's wish. I could have gone, but my mother became so upset at the thought of being left alone that the opportunity was allowed to slip by.

The memory of those days and the day of the funeral in particular are hazy. One's thoughts were too unhappy to be preserved with any permanence, and the sequence of events has become rather blurred in the fifty odd years that have passed. At the time the mind recalled events of the more recent past – the days sailing off Deal in Baker's yawl, a friendly argument about a move on the chess board, and above all a conversation one evening soon after the death of J. B. Pinker. I forget now how this started but I remember the gist of JC's remarks at the time, and have had cause to be grateful for the courage they have given me in later years. Though they were said in my presence, I had the impression that he was speaking as much to himself as to me.

7. 5. 23.

6. pm.

EFFENDI HILL
OYSTER BAY, LONG ISLAND
NEW YORK

My dearest John.
Your letter (and mother's)
have been delayed and
have just arrived.
The packet sails tomorrow
and I have only just
time to thank you
and send you my
dear love. I think
of you with affection and
confidence
Your devoted father

PS. tell Mother you hear from me.

Copy of the only remaining letter from Joseph Conrad to John

'When a friend dies one pictures, as it were, the marching columns of humanity as they proceed from the cradle to the grave, moving on, day by day, inexorably. Each morning one casts a look around to see if all ones friends are there; the older ones go on ahead, the younger ones follow behind and if all are there one is content. Then one is missing from his usual place – there is an unfilled space which remains for the rest of your life. More spaces appear to remain unoccupied; you look along the column calling to your mind the name of those who have gone on. You remember them all, the good, the bad, the sad and the cheerful and are thankful that you can recall the past; happy for those released from a life of pain, sad at the unexpected passing and above all thankful for the blessing you have received from "The Good Lord".'